C000178731

The Vulcan B.Mk2
from a Different Angle

CRAIG BULMAN

With compliments

Craig Bulman

10.03.08

Pentland Books

© C. Bulman 2001
First published in 2001 by
Pentland Books Ltd
1 Hutton Close
South Church
Bishop Auckland
Durham
DL14 6XB

manuscripts@pentlandpress.co.uk
sales@pentlandpress.co.uk
Web:www.pentlandpress.co.uk

All rights reserved
Unauthorised duplication
contravenes existing laws
It is the moral right of the author
to be associated with this work

ISBN 1 85821 899 3

Typeset in Helvetica [titles] and Dante 11 on 14 by
Carnegie Publishing Ltd
Carnegie House
Chatsworth Road
Lancaster
LA1 4SL

www.carnegiepub.co.uk

Printed and bound in the UK by
Cromwell Press Ltd, Trowbridge, Wilts

Front and rear cover photo: *Four Vulcan B.Mk2s (XL392, XM574, XL446 and XL426) of No. 617 Sqn on detachment to RAF Leeming on 16 October 1979.* (**Author's collection**)

Inside front cover: *Equipped with a Blue Steel missile is XL321 of No. 617 Sqn on 18 July 1962.* (**CBV**)

Title page: *Although the serial number of this Vulcan appears to be unidentifiable, by studying the features and modifications on the aircraft it is possible to create a shortlist of just five: XH557, XJ784, XM645, XM646 or XM647. The Vulcan depicted in this impressive low-level run at Biggin Hill on 18 September 1971 is in fact XM645 of the Waddington Wing.* (**QAPI**)

Inside back cover: *XM650 of the Waddington Wing c.1968–71. Note the tip of the 'X band jammer' directly above the end of the exhaust pipe.* (**CBV**)

Rear cover-inside of the sleeve: *The author reoccupies the Nav Radar's seat inside the cockpit of XL388 at the Blyth Valley Aviation Collection.* (**Author's collection**)

£15-

The Vulcan B.Mk2 from a Different Angle

Contents

Vulcan B.Mk2 Production

Production number:	Serial number:	Production number:	Serial number:	Production number:	Serial number:
1	XH533	31	XL359	61	XM597
2	XH534	32	XL360	62	XM598
3	XH535	33	XL361	63	XM599
4	XH536	34	XL384	64	XM600
5	XH537	35	XL385	65	XM601
6	XH538	36	XL386	66	XM602
7	XH539	37	XL387	67	XM603
8	XH554	38	XL388	68	XM604
9	XH555	39	XL389	69	XM605
10	XH556	40	XL390	70	XM606
11	XH557	41	XL391	71	XM607
12	XH558	42	XL392	72	XM608
13	XH559	43	XL425	73	XM609
14	XH560	44	XL426	74	XM610
15	XH561	45	XL427	75	XM611
16	XH562	46	XL443	76	XM612
17	XH563	47	XL444	77	XM645
18	XJ780	48	XL445	78	XM646
19	XJ781	49	XL446	79	XM647
20	XJ782	50	XM569	80	XM648
21	XJ783	51	XM570	81	XM649
22	XJ784	52	XM571	82	XM650
23	XJ823	53	XM572	83	XM651
24	XJ824	54	XM573	84	XM652
25	XJ825	55	XM574	85	XM653
26	XL317	56	XM575	86	XM654
27	XL318	57	XM576	87	XM655
28	XL319	58	XM594	88	XM656
29	XL320	59	XM595	89	XM657
30	XL321	60	XM596*	* fatigue test airframe	

Acknowledgements

IN ORDER TO PROVIDE A WIDER SELECTION of photographic material for this book I have called upon many people who have thankfully agreed to share their valued possession of photographs. First, I acknowledge the time and effort taken by John Hoggon, who has delved deep into his files to bring together a fine selection of material. The following ex-Vulcan crew members have provided further contributions, including reference dates/photographs:

Alan Chapman (Captain)

Colin N. Dodds (Captain)

John Hatherway (AEO)

Pete Odling (Captain)

Mike Pollit (Pilot)

Rod Powell (AEO)

L. D. A. Rusty Russell (Captain)

Additional photographs and technical details, together with advice and guidance, have been provided by:

Dave Belston (Crown Copyright)

Stuart H. Bourne (Quality Aviation Photos International — QAPI)

Les Bulman

Eddie and Sue Clark

Steven Connor

Colin J. Dodds

Andrew Edmondson (Vulcan Operating Company, Project Manager — XH558)

Eric Graham

Derek Hammond (655 MaPS, Maintenance and Preservation Society — XM655)

Paul Hartley (655 MaPS)

John Hemingbrough

Nigel Horn (Vulcan Operating Company — XH558)

Craig Jackson

Mark Keating (Carnegie Publishing)

Colin King (Vulcan Restoration Trust — XL426)

Russell Kirk (Lincolnshire Echo)

Geoff Penn (Vulcan Restoration Trust — XL426)

Terry Quinn

Andrew Simpson (Curator, Royal Air Force Museum)

Brian Stainer (Aviation Photo News — APN)

Ken Thompson

Richard Triner

Andy Vass (Vulcan Restoration Trust — XL426)

Andrew Ward (655 MaPS)

I thank all of the above for their patience during the persistent telephone calls and generosity for giving freely their time, photographs, information and advice. Some people have played a larger part than others, but even the smallest contributions are greatly appreciated.

Kaye Thompson (Publishing Manager) and Grace Crisholm (Executive Editor) of Pentland Books are both thanked for their help in the publication of this book.

Last but not least thanks are given to Karen for her patience and understanding and for having to live in a house that looks like it has been hit by a Blue Steel missile (rooms littered with books, photographs and mounds of paper).

Introduction

THROUGHOUT MY LIFE I HAVE LIVED in and around the industrial town of Middlesborough in the North East of England. During my teenage years in the 1970s I used to look forward to the sight or sound of the next passing aircraft. Among the regular daily sightings were the Jet Provosts from RAF Leeming and Linton On Ouse. Looking to the south-east in the direction of Scarborough approximately fifty miles away, you could get your first glimpse of the vapour trails given off by the airliners on their transatlantic flights between Europe and North America. These airliners, which included Boeing 707s, 747s, McDonnell Douglas DC8s, DC10s and Illusion IL62s, would pass by Teesside as they made their way along the Yorkshire coast at about 31,000 ft. The most memorable sights by far, however, were the Vulcan Bombers from Lincolnshire. The Vulcans were routinely seen at altitude heading north-bound as they passed over the North Yorkshire moors and then over and beyond Teesside. All activities would stop as either myself or one of my friends would shout, 'there's a vapour trail' or 'it's a Vulcan'. When the weather conditions were good and you could clearly see the underside of the Vulcan against a blue sky, nothing could take away the sense of pride as this truly British aircraft of the Royal Air Force went about its training to maintain the deterrent. With the aid of binoculars or a telescope my eyes would be transfixed on the aircraft's large delta wing as it passed gracefully overhead. Whilst admiring the shape of the leading edge of the wing and the engine nestles protruding beneath the inner wing, it eventually became apparent that not all of the Vulcans were the same. Noticeable differences included a large flat panel between one or both pairs of engines. Further study revealed that the silver exhaust pipes were in two different sizes, apparently indicating the series of Olympus engines that the individual aircraft had fitted to them.

Air Shows from then on proved to be more exciting as each Vulcan was given a far more detailed inspection of airframe and markings. Over the coming years further examinations revealed more differences and some Vulcans were noted as transferring between different Units more frequently than others. During 1979 with the help of my friends we recorded every Vulcan that we saw passing over Teesside. On 19 June 1979, over seven hours, we spotted twenty-two Vulcans flying at approximately 32,000–35,000 ft. The biggest surprise came on 26 November 1979 at 14:24 hours when I looked through the binoculars at a Vulcan heading northbound (about 32,000 ft) and I shouted, 'it's got missiles under its wings'. In due course we were to discover that these were in fact air-sampling pods, which were fitted to some of No. 27 Sqn's B.Mk2 MRRs (I wonder what the serial number of that aircraft was?).

The day I always looked forward to more than any other was the annual Waddington Open Day. During June 1980 I had to make the biggest decision of my life, whether to sacrifice the Open Day in order to represent the Central and East Yorkshire Wing of the Air Training Corps at the Class C High Jump held at RAF Cranwell, which fell on the same weekend. In the end I sacrificed my day with the Vulcans, believing that attending the Open Day would have been a purely selfish act (surely the interests of my Squadron and Wing should come first). The outcome was a gold medal in the event, resulting in automatic selection to represent the region at RAF Cosford at a later date.

Climbing aboard XL388 on 2 April 1982 is the author, followed by Flt Lt M. R. Aston of No. 50 Sqn (AEO). **(Author's collection)**

My greatest ambition had always been to be up there inside one of the Vulcans, as opposed to remaining with my feet on the ground acting only as an enthusiast/observer. This ambition was fulfilled in 1982 whilst I was a Cadet Warrant Officer in the ATC (1869 Middlesborough Squadron). After initially making contact with No. 617 Sqn, I was sent to RAF North Luffenham to receive the training in order to obtain an aeromedical certificate. Owing to the fact that the famous Dambuster squadron was about to disband, my details were transferred to No. 50 Sqn at Waddington. After years of only dreaming, Wednesday, 31 March 1982 was to be the big day. The next step was to climb aboard the unidentified B.Mk1A

nose section inside one of Waddington's hangars to receive the necessary training on how to abandon the aircraft in case of an emergency. The original planned flight in Vulcan B.Mk2 XH561 was cancelled and instead I climbed aboard XL426 that evening to join the crew which conducted a CT (Circuit Training) sortie over the Lincolnshire countryside and around Waddington.

The station's Community Relations Officer Flt Lt Michael Fogarty then made arrangements for a further two-day stay, as No. 50 Sqn had given me the opportunity to take a further flight on Friday, 2 April 1982. The flight would be made in XL388, as it was destined to serve the remainder of its time on the fire dump at RAF Honington. On Thursday 1 April I was invited aboard XM569 as it taxied up the eastern taxiway and back down runway 21 to ascertain the extent of a perceived problem with the nose wheel steering. I recall looking out of the circular side observation window and seeing the numerous Vulcans sitting silently on their dispersals as we taxied past, knowing that their service life was about to end. When this aircraft returned from a sortie later that day I was invited to climb aboard for a further CT sortie, but this was cancelled because one of the crew was feeling ill. The following morning I became the fifth member of the crew of XL388 and on that occasion I occupied the Nav Radar's seat on the left. Upon arrival at Honington the remaining fuel was burnt off by conducting further touch-and-go circuits. I vividly remember seeing the flight line of Tornado aircraft of the Tactical Weapons Unit positioned on the main apron, knowing that they were the intended replacement for the highly respected and well loved Vulcan Bomber.

Although this was the eleventh hour of the Vulcan Bomber, whilst XL388 was in the Honington circuit, the Argentine forces were in the process of capturing the Falkland Islands. The remaining Vulcans were given a temporary reprieve and remained in service for a little longer.

This book concentrates on the individual Vulcan B.Mk2s, first by sequencing chronologically all of the appropriate aircraft allocated to the squadrons/Units that collectively built up the Bomber Wings at the RAF stations. This provides a far more clear and comprehensive picture about which aircraft serial numbers and occasionally production batches were used at the appropriate times to equip the various Units/Wings. To a certain degree it is possible to determine 'why' these aircraft were transferred from and to different Units at a particular point in time.

Second, the book describes numerous original features and modifications, and then lists all the aircraft with that particular feature. There are multitudes of permutations due to each aircraft receiving a percentage but not all of the modifications during its years of service. Certain modifications however were applied to all aircraft over time, and on those occasions the book quotes the approximate date that a particular feature was first noted and the date at which it appears to have become universal. By process of elimination it is possible to identify an individual aircraft/production batch even though it is not possible to see the aircraft's serial number.

Taking all of this into account, much more of the history of the Vulcan Bomber remains to be told. As more information is discovered and further stories are told, a far more detailed and fuller account of this magnificent aircraft will be possible.

The dates quoted within this book showing the transfer or allocation of an aircraft from one Unit to another may differ slightly from the date that the actual physical movement occurred.

Details of allocation to squadrons/Units may show discrepancies due to the fact that aircraft visits to St Athan for major servicing, sometimes for a couple of months, are too numerous to mention.

Copyright owner of (CBV) is of unknown authorship. All reasonable enquiries have been made to determine copyright ownership of this material, however it is believed that the material may be Crown Copyright.

Photographs acknowledged as (RAAF Copyright Reserved) or (Crown Copyright/MOD) have been reproduced with the permission of Her Majesty's Stationery Office.

Development and Training

P RIOR TO THE FIRST VULCAN B.MKI AIRCREW being trained by
No. 230 OCU, Bristol Siddeley was already developing an Olympus
engine producing around 16,000 lb of thrust with the potential to
achieve up to 20,000 lb. This was in comparison with 13,500 lb offered by the
earlier Olympus 104s of the B.Mk1. The new engine would require an
increase in mass air flow of 700 lb per second at sea level, which could be
achieved by increasing the size of the air intakes. In order to gain the full
potential from the new engine, the basic airframe and electrical systems of
the B.Mk1 would require redesigning, with particular attention given to the
aircraft's wing. What became known as the phase 2C wing with its distinc-
tive 'kinked' leading edge, rounded wing-tips and overall greater size resulting from a 12 ft increase in span (99 to 111 ft). These features would improve
the range of the aircraft and increase performance at altitude by allowing
the Vulcan to climb above 60,000 ft. The aircraft would also be given an
extended, bulged tail cone to accommodate a vast array of electronic coun-
termeasures. The new version of the Vulcan would be known as the B.Mk2.

The phase 2C wing was first flown on 31 August 1957 after being fitted to the second Mk1 prototype VX777, which then became the prototype for the B.Mk2. VX777 appeared at the Farnborough SBAC display
that year and went on to serve in a programme of trials for a further six
years, before being broken up at Farnborough in July 1963.

As a result of the improved performance offered by the B.Mk2, it
seemed appropriate to reduce the numbers of the earlier Mk1 Vulcans
already on order by changing the production line to the new version. It
was also important to get the Mk2 Vulcans into squadron service as soon
as possible, so the final twenty-four B.Mk1s on order were then built as
B.Mk2s (XH533–9, XH554–63, XJ780–4 and XJ823–5).

Before the B.Mk2 could enter squadron service with the RAF, extensive flight trials were required (A&AEE), followed by aircrew training

which would be carried out by No. 230 OCU. In order to get the first pre-production aircraft into the air as soon as possible, XH533 would lack many of the B.Mk2s features. This aircraft took to the air on 19 August 1958 still retaining its pointed Mk1 tail cone but fitted with Olympus 200 series engines producing 16,000 lb of thrust. The urgency to get XH533 into the air is indicated by the fact that it was not until February 1959 before the last production B.Mk1 (XH532) was completed. The attention of Avro had now been directed towards XH534, which would be far more representative of the definitive B.Mk2 by having a flight-refuelling probe fitted along with the new bulged ECM tail cone and 201 series engines (17,000 lb). The third production aircraft XH535 served for four years at the A&AEE from 27 May 1960 to 5 May 1964. During that time this air-craft was involved in numerous trials, which included among others the Auxiliary Airborne Power Plant, ECM, radio and electromagnetic com-patibility trials for the Skybolt missile. Unfortunately this aircraft was written-off on 5 May 1964 when it crashed at Chute near Andover in Wiltshire after going into a spin whilst attempting a high rate of descent approach at low speed to Boscombe Down. After being delivered on 16 December 1959, XH536 was initially used by Controller (Aircraft) and then by the Ministry of Aviation as a test bed for the Olympus 200 series engine. The next two Vulcan B.Mk2s awaiting collection from the manu-facturers were to assist in the trials of the Skybolt missile (XH537 27 August 1959 and XH538 23 September 1959). Initially the latter aircraft was fitted with a flight-refuelling probe (later removed c.1962) whilst two small blisters on the top of its nose and darker red/white/blue national markings could identify the former aircraft. Both XH537 and XH538 had three small black-and-white fairings fitted beneath the outer wing-tips and to the rear of the nose wheel doors, which housed cameras. By 1962

Figure 1.1:
To get the Vulcan B.Mk2 into service as soon as possible, most of the early production aircraft were used on devel-opment/trials work. One of these was XH539, which initially conducted trials with the Blue Steel missile. The aircraft is seen here later in its career at Boscombe Down (notice the fairing protruding from the rear of the bomb aiming blister which contains a camera pointing to the rear). (APN)

both aircraft had received the bulged ECM tail cone, although XH537 still lacked the wing-tip dielectric panels. Trials on the Blue Steel missile were to be conducted by XH539 (awaiting collection 30 September 1959), with some assistance from XH538.

The next three aircraft, XH554, XH555 and XH556, were not available to enter service until 1961 (10 April, 14 July and 29 September respectively). When XH554 finally entered service it still had the shallower air intakes of the B.Mk1. XH557 first flew on 21 June 1960 and was later used in trials of the Olympus 301 engines (20,000 lb), but only after modifications to its engine bays. This aircraft came off the production line with the wider air intakes, which became standard on all the B.Mk2s. Although some of these earlier B.Mk2 aircraft originally had the Mk1 tail cone, they all eventually received the bulged ECM tail. Only three of these Vulcans, XH533, XH535 and XH539, did not enter squadron service.

During the early months of 1960, XH534 had undergone official CA release trials at Boscombe Down and, as a result, in May 1960 the B.Mk2 was finally given the CA clearance and could enter service. The first seven production aircraft (XH533–9) had all contributed to clearance testing at Boscombe Down at various times.

On 1 July 1960 at RAF Waddington in Lincolnshire, the RAF took delivery of its first Vulcan B.Mk2 when XH558 joined 'B' Flight of No. 230 OCU ('A' Flight operated the B.Mk1). The following month XH559 arrived to join 'B' Flight of the OCU on 24 August 1960. On 3 October the OCU received its third B.Mk2, XH560, followed by XH561, which arrived just over a month later (11 November 1960). After being allocated XH562 on 9 December, the OCU would have had five B.Mk2s, but things did not go according to plan. When these service aircraft were flying at medium-to-high altitude, the Olympus 201 engines appeared to be surge prone when double handling, which was followed by flameouts. Owing to the paired engines sharing the same air intake, the pressure disturbance after an engine flameout was reflected into the second engine, occasionally resulting in the loss of two engines. Although the Olympus engines would relight easily, these circumstances were unacceptable to the RAF. Having suffered several flameouts during its eight weeks in service, XH560 was returned to Avro to allow the company to investigate the problem. It must have been an enormous task for personnel within the OCU to keep its four remaining Vulcan B.Mk2s serviceable so that instructors could train new aircrew for No. 83 Sqn. This squadron was now being equipped with the B.Mk2 (XH563 28 December 1960, XJ780 16 January, XJ781 23 February, XJ782 2 March, XJ783 13 March and XH554 10 April 1961). On 29 March 1961 XJ784 was issued to the Ministry of Aviation to assist in further trials.

On 18 June 1961 No. 230 OCU moved across to Yorkshire to RAF Finningley, whilst No. 101 Sqn made the reverse move, taking its five B.Mk1s and two B.Mk1As to Waddington. Apart from those allocated to the OCU, all of the B.Mk1s and B.Mk1As would now be concentrated at Waddington.

By October 1961 No. 27 Sqn had also established itself at RAF Scampton operating five B.Mk2s (XJ823 21 April, XJ824 16 May, XH555 14 July, XJ825 28 July and XH556 29 September 1961). The next task of the OCU would have been to train the crews for No. 617 Sqn at Scampton. It was important to get Blue Steel into service as soon as possible now that the B.Mk2 was finally operational with Nos 27 and 83 Sqns. It was only after the next eight aircraft had been delivered to No. 617 Sqn that the OCU received an increase in its allocation. XL384 was allocated to 'B' Flight of No. 230 OCU on 2 April 1962.

By this time all of the Vulcans on the OCU displayed on the tail fin the white Yorkshire Rose on a light blue background. Throughout the remainder of 1962 three more Vulcan B.Mk2s joined the OCU. XL387 arrived from Woodford on 4 June with XL389 joining on 13 July. These were followed by XH554 transferring from No. 83 Sqn on 1 November 1962, after being replaced on that squadron by the arrival of additional Blue Steel aircraft, e.g. XL443 8 October 1962. After receiving XL389 from AVRO at Woodford, all future Vulcans joining the OCU would be transferred from other Units.

As No. 27 Sqn converted to Blue Steel, its earlier Vulcans operating in the free-fall bombing role were distributed to other Units. By the end of spring 1963, No. 230 OCU had taken charge of XH555 and XH556. This would have increased the total number of B.Mk2s to ten, but XH554 had returned to Avro (6 March 1963) and XH562 transferred to the newly reformed No. 35 Sqn at RAF Coningsby (1 March 1963). XH554 remained at Woodford for twenty months before being returned to service, presumably to have its air intakes widened, as well as receiving a manufacturer's retrofit (updated and additional equipment, e.g. radars and jammers). XH562 initially served at Coningsby for only ten days before returning to the OCU to serve for a further seven weeks until finally joining No. 35 Sqn on 30 April 1963. The following day XH561 was involved in a Cat 3R FA (1 May), but after receiving repairs was soon returned to service assisting in the training of more aircrew. By mid-September XH558 had been observed fitted with a flight-refuelling probe.

Starting in August 1963 the individual aircraft allocated to the OCU were shuffled around, with some of the Vulcans being returned to Avro at Woodford for a manufacturer's retrofit and modification work. In order to maintain the Unit's numbers, additional Vulcans were sent to join the OCU for varying periods until they themselves required a retrofit. On 7 August 1963 both XH559 and XL384 made their way to Woodford whilst in return XJ780 was transferred from the Coningsby Wing (16 August 1963). Making another appearance on the OCU was XH562, which rejoined the Unit on 19 September 1963. After a three-year absence, XH560 returned to the OCU, but this time the Unit was stationed at Finningley (29 November 1963). Both XJ780 and XH560 had transferred from No. 12 Sqn. The next six Vulcan B.Mk2s joining the OCU also came from the Coningsby Wing, as they had all been replaced one by one with the introduction into service of new 301 series aircraft equipped to carry Skybolt. On 2 December 1963 XL387 departed for Woodford and on the same day XJ824 arrived from No. 9 Sqn to take its place. Eighteen days later XJ782 arrived at Finningley to join 'B' Flight of the OCU (20 December 1963). On 4 February 1964, the youngest aircraft within the OCU departed for Woodford (XL389) and taking its place on the same day was XJ781. A further exchange took place in February, with XH558 leaving on the 11th and XJ783 arriving from No. 9 Sqn on the 28th. XJ783 would have arrived a few days earlier but it had been involved in a Cat 3R flying accident the previous week. At the end of February 1964 the current amount of aircraft allocated to the OCU was ten (XH555, XH556, XH560–2, XJ780–3 and XJ824).

During 1964 the scene at all of the V-Bomber stations started to change dramatically. The white aircraft that stood out in stark contrast to the airfield's surroundings would soon have their upper surfaces painted in green and grey camouflage, as the V-Force changed to low-level

Figure 1.2: Members of the Air Training Corps during their annual camp, which include those of No. 1869 Middlesborough Squadron, in front of XJ780 from No. 230 OCU at RAF Finningley on 3 September 1963. Note the smooth under-wing surface below the two black marks on the leading edge of the wing. Even though the Skybolt missile project had been cancelled in November 1962, this aircraft, along with some others, received wing-attachment points (twin blisters) during 1964/65. **(Crown Copyright/ MOD)**

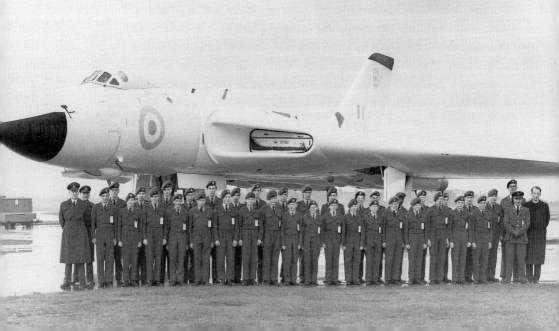

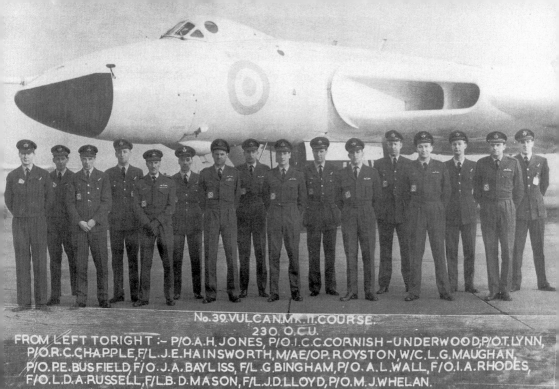

No. 39. VULCAN MK. II. COURSE.
230. O.C.U.
FROM LEFT TO RIGHT :– P/O.A.H.JONES, P/O.I.C.C.CORNISH –UNDERWOOD,P/O.T.LYNN, P/O.R.C.CHAPPLE,F/L.J.E.HAINSWORTH, M/AE/OP. ROYSTON,W/C.L.G.MAUGHAN, P/O.P.E.BUSFIELD, F/O.J.A.BAYLISS, F/L.G.BINGHAM,P/O. A.L.WALL, F/O.I.A.RHODES, F/O.L.D.A.RUSSELL, F/L.B.D.MASON, F/L.J.D.LLOYD, P/O.M.J.WHELAN.

operations. Centralized servicing was also adopted resulting in the removal of the individual Unit markings from the aircraft's tail fin. No. 230 OCU removed the Yorkshire rose from the tail fin and the Unit crest on the forward fuselage and applied its official badge, depicting a golden sword on a blue wave background, onto the crew entrance door. A number of the earlier aircraft such as XJ781, XJ782 and XJ783 appeared with this marking on the entrance door whilst still in their original white colour scheme (1964).

After serving at Finningley for seven months, XJ780 left 'B' Flight to receive a manufacture's retrofit, commencing on 2 March 1964. One month later on 2 April XH562 also left for a retrofit. On the last day of April, XJ825 (ex-No. 35 Sqn) arrived from Coningsby to join the OCU followed on 11 May by XJ823 also from No. 35 Sqn. In the meantime, on 6 May, XH559 returned to the Unit after a retrofit. Twenty-two days later on 2 June XH560 departed to the manufacturers to receive a retrofit. On 24 June XJ823 departed Finningley and flew about thirty-six miles northeast to RAF Leconfield, where it remained for nine days with No.60 Maintenance Unit before being returned to the OCU on 2 July displaying the new green and grey camouflage. This new look was on display to the public nine days later (11 July) when XJ823 was part of the static display at RAF Abingdon's Open Day. After serving for just under four months, XJ825 left 'B' Flight of the OCU for a retrofit (18 August 1964). XJ783

Figure 1.3:
This picture, taken at RAF Finningley on 6 January 1964, shows No. 39 Vulcan B.Mk2 Course (5 December 1963– 2 April 1964). Although the Vulcan has yet to be positively identified, the only aircraft known to have been equipped with a flight-refuelling probe whilst operating with the OCU at that time was XH558. **(Crown Copyright/ MOD)**

became the next B.Mk2 to leave the Unit, departing on 25 September 1964 (manufacturer's retrofit). After a twenty-month absence, XH554 returned to Finningley on 5 November 1964 where it was destined to remain, attached to No. 230 OCU, for the next sixteen-and-a-half years. By the end of 1964 there were nine B.Mk2s allocated to the OCU (XH554–6, XH559, XH561, XJ781, XJ782, XJ823 and XJ824).

On 15 January 1965 XH561 was involved in a further Cat 3R flying accident after making a wheels-up landing at its home base. It eventually returned to service, after receiving repairs, and continued to operate with the OCU. During March two more Vulcans were stood down from the OCU to receive manufacturer's retrofits (XJ781, 1 March 1965 and XJ782, 29 March 1965). Joining the Unit for the first time (6 March) having just received a retrofit was XH563 (ex-No.12 Sqn). Two months later, it became the turn of XJ824 to leave for retrofit (28 May 1965) but to make the numbers back up again, Finningley received the two ex-Skybolt Vulcans (XH537 and XH538) which both arrived on 31 May. Two further Vulcans left the OCU during the following month, with both of the aircraft departing on 28 June (XH554 and XJ823). The first of these two Vulcans, XH554, was away for only two months to receive manufacturer's modifications, whilst the latter was absent for fourteen months receiving a retrofit. A day later, on 29 June, XH558 returned to service after retrofit. This was the very first Vulcan B.Mk2 that had entered service with the RAF five years previously. On 26 July, after the completion of the manufacturer's retrofit, XJ780 returned to service with the OCU, followed by XH554 arriving on 2 September. Shortly after, XH537 was absent from Finningley for three months (23 September–13 December 1965) receiving manufacturer's modifications. When it returned to the OCU in December, the total number of B.Mk2s allocated to the Unit was ten (XH537, XH538, XH554–6, XH558, XH559, XH561, XH563 and XJ780).

Figure 1.4:
XJ780 seen after being retrofitted with the twin (Skybolt) attachment points, identified by the two blisters/fairings under the wing.
(APN)

Figure 1.5:
XH558 of No. 230
OCU at Finningley
(c.1965). Notice the
very small 'IFF'
(Identified Friend or
Foe) aerial on top of
the fuselage, behind
the much larger UHF
aerial. (APN)

Over the past five-and-a-half years all of the Vulcan B.Mk2s operating with No. 230 OCU were fitted with Olympus 201 series engines. These aircraft by now were all painted in the two-tone camouflage and had each been fitted with a flight-refuelling probe. By the end of 1965 the OCU had relinquished the last two of its B.Mk1s, when XA900 was issued to No. 2 SoTT at Cosford and XA901 was flown to Cranwell. Both of these aircraft left the OCU on 19 November 1965 and unfortunately they were eventually scrapped (1986 and 1972 respectively).

Throughout 1966 the previously mentioned ten B.Mk2s continued to serve with the OCU, apart from XH561, which had left on 28 March to receive a manufacturer's retrofit. All was going well at Finningley until 18 April when suddenly, as XH556 started up its engines for a routine training sortie, the aircraft's undercarriage collapsed. After a detailed inspection XH556 was struck off charge and placed on to the Finningley dump.

On 18 June 1966 XL444, which had been part of the Scampton Wing for the past three-and-a-half years, transferred across to Finningley to serve with the OCU for the next twelve months before returning to Scampton on 19 June 1967. Eight weeks after XL444 had joined the OCU, XJ823 returned to Finningley to rejoin the Unit once again (12 August 1966). XJ823 served for only three months before being issued to the Waddington Wing on 1 November 1966. After serving as a development aircraft since 1959, XH534 finally entered service with the RAF when it joined No. 230 OCU on 6 December 1966. Nine days later XH558 departed to receive the necessary manufacturer's modifications, before returning on 23 February 1967. In December, a further aircraft was allocated to the OCU, but with a difference. XJ784 arrived at Finningley (22 December 1966) to become the first Vulcan to be operated by the OCU fitted with

Figure 1.6:
A superb shot of
XH555 of No. 230
OCU just after take-
off at Wethersfield
on 11 June 1966.
(APN)

the more powerful Olympus 301 series engines. This aircraft became the second B.Mk2 to have its engine bays modified to accept the 301 series engines in April 1962, whilst it had been serving as a development aircraft at the A&AEE.

During 1967, most of the Vulcans currently on strength remained with the Unit for the full twelve months (XH534, XH537, XH538, XH554, XH555, XH559, XH563 and XJ784). When XH558 arrived back in February, it too continued with the OCU throughout the remainder of 1967. XJ780, on the other hand, received manufacturer modifications from 7 March to 17 May 1967, then returned to the OCU for a further five months before being issued to the Waddington Wing on 10 October 1967. As previously mentioned, XL444 also left the Unit on 19 June 1967. With only three days remaining of 1967, XL446 (ex-Waddington Wing) joined the OCU after receiving its manufacturer's modifications (2 November 1967–28 December 1967). Allegedly operating with the OCU for two months from 7 August to 1 October 1967 was XM609 from the Cottesmore Wing.

In 1968 three aircraft left the OCU, with XH538 initially receiving manufacturer's modifications commencing on 12 August 1968, before joining the Scampton Wing in May 1969. The other two aircraft both joined the Waddington Wing, starting with XH558 on 26 February and followed by XH563 on 6 August 1968. In exchange for XH563, the OCU received from the Waddington Wing XM645 with its 301 series engines on 5 August 1968. The latter aircraft received manufacturer's modifications from 1 November–9 December 1968. Two more of the Unit's Vulcans were away from Finningley receiving manufacturer's modifications during 1968, namely XH534 (1 March–3 May 1968) and XL446 (31 May–2 July

1968). Earlier in the year XM573 transferred across from Waddington (15 February 1968), possibly in exchange for XH558, which, as already indicated, made the move to Waddington eleven days later. By the end of the year the following nine aircraft were allocated to the OCU: XH534, XH537, XH554, XH555, XH559, XJ784, XL446, XM573 and XM645.

There was one reported mishap for the OCU in 1968, when XH555 sustained some structural damage after making a heavy landing at Finningley. Although this incident is shown as occurring during 1968, XH555 remained in service with the OCU into the following year. The Chief Flying Instructor on the OCU at that time was Sqn Ldr Peter Odling, who had flown XH555 on seven occasions during 1968/69, the last of these flights occurring on 13 March 1969. Odling had first flown in XH555 as a Flt Lt on 15 November 1963 when he was originally attached to the OCU; he later transferred to the Scampton Wing flying Blue Steel operations. The exact date of the heavy landing still remains unknown, but what is known is that after the incident the aircraft was then declared Cat 5 and used for fatigue and structural testing by the manufacturers until being struck off charge on 10 October 1971 and eventually scrapped.

No. 230 OCU continued to operate a total of nine Vulcan B.Mk2s during 1969 until the previously mentioned incident with XH555 occurred. By the end of the year, the only other change to the OCU's compliment of aircraft was XH563 in place of XH559. The former aircraft (XH563) returned from Waddington on 18 March 1969 (loaned to Min-Tech on two occasions, 8 April–11 June and 18 September–2 October 1969) whilst the latter aircraft was away at Hawker Siddeley's facility at Bitteswell receiving manufacturer's modifications (4 August 1969–27 February 1970). The following two aircraft both received modification work during

Figure 1.7:
On display inside one of RAF Finningley's hangars on 17 September 1966 is XH554, poised and ready to demonstrate an undercarriage retraction test. Notice the OCU insignia along with the station badge on the crew entrance door and the aircraft's serial number on the inside of the main undercarriage door.
(John Hemingbrough)

Craig Bulman

Figure 1.8:
Whilst at Offutt AFB
on 19 May 1968, Sqn
Ldr Peter Odling
(Chief Flying
Instructor No. 230
OCU) flying XH559
demonstrates to this
American audience
(all giving complete
attention) the power
of the Vulcan B.Mk2
and how effortlessly
it can get into the air.
Also noticeable are
the 'three' smoke
trails from the
Olympus engines,
which are due to the
fitting of modified
fuel cans (burners)
on one of the engines
in an attempt to
reduce smoke emis-
sions (1968).
(Omaha World
Herald)

the year: XH537 (27 February–2 April 1969) and XJ784 (12 May–13 June 1969).

In December 1969 the scene around Doncaster was about to change in a big way. The people living in and around the town had witnessed the sight and sound of the Vulcan Bombers for the past twelve years (No. 101 Sqn, October 1957), but this was to be no more. The OCU was to move to what then became its third station at RAF Scampton in Lincolnshire whilst operating these aircraft. By the time XH559 had returned to service at the end of February, there were nine Vulcan B.Mk2s allocated to the OCU at Scampton (XH534, XH537, XH554, XH559, XH563, XJ784, XL446, XM573 and XM645).

At the beginning of the 1970s the circumstances within the V-Force had changed owing to the introduction of Polaris in 1969 (No. 83 Sqn had disbanded and No. 27 Sqn had converted to free-fall bombing). No. 617 Sqn was the sole remaining Unit operating Blue Steel, although it too was due to relinquish the Stand Off missile and convert to free-fall bombing at the end of 1970. This meant that after the Vulcans themselves had been converted back to free-fall bombing, there would be a surplus number of aircraft available to distribute to the remaining Units.

On 1 April 1970 the first of these ex-Blue Steel aircraft, XL386, joined the OCU. This was followed on 14 May 1970 by XL319, which also transferred to the OCU. Two further aircraft were allocated to the OCU during the year, namely XL361 on 7 October and XL384 on 27 November 1970. For just a couple of weeks at a time, XL389 and XL392 were both operated by the OCU (1 November–December and 11–21 December respectively). Two of the Unit's Vulcans were to leave Scampton and transfer to the sunnier climate of Cyprus to join the NEAF (XM573 on

26 June and XJ784 on 21 July 1970). By the end of 1970 the Vulcans on strength with the OCU were: XH534, XH537, XH554, XH559, XH563, XL319, XL361, XL384, XL386, XL446 and XM645 (eleven in total). Also worth noting at this point is that the RAF had seventy-eight Vulcan B.Mk2s available to distribute between the seven squadrons and the OCU (with the exception of XH539, which was still operating with the A&AEE at Boscombe Down). Taking into account the aircraft that would have been out of service for manufacturer's modifications at St Athan and Bitteswell, and then allocating eight aircraft to each Unit (sixty-four in total), there still would have been a surplus. This probably accounts for the high allocation to No. 230 OCU and also the slight increase in numbers operating with the NEAF in Cyprus at that time.

During 1971 four of the Unit's aircraft — XH534, XH537, XH559 and XL386 — continued to operate with it for the full twelve months. Although XL446 served alongside throughout the year, it left the OCU on 15 December 1971 to receive manufacturer's modifications (completed 18 April 1972). This aircraft was then returned to service at Scampton for three months, by which time No. 27 Sqn had disbanded, leaving only No. 617 Sqn and No. 230 OCU as the only Units stationed there. XH554 also served throughout the year, apart from an absence of four months for manufacturer's modifications (17 March–27 July 1972). In April 1971 there were a number of changes with XL388 arriving from the Scampton Wing on the 19th and XH538 returning on the 21st after a two-and-a-half-year absence. Two of the Vulcans leaving the scene were XM645 and XL319 on the 21st and 22nd respectively. XM645 returned to Waddington, whilst XL319 transferred to No. 617 Sqn. Another OCU aircraft, XL361, left on the 4th for five weeks to be used by the two squadrons making up the Scampton Wing at that time, but was returned on 12 May 1971. Four further aircraft were operated by the OCU during May (XL390 30 April–3 June, XL444 5 April–11 May, XM574 3–12 May and XM575 3–7 May).

After being one of the last Vulcans to be equipped with Blue Steel in 1970, XL360 returned to service with No. 617 Sqn in the free-fall bombing role in May 1971 before transferring to the OCU on 13 July 1971. Exactly one month later on 13 August XL361 departed to receive manufacturer's modifications, which took until 29 December 1971 to complete, before being returned to the OCU.

On 12 August 1971 XL384 was grounded after making a heavy landing at Scampton. The following day the aircraft was assessed as Cat 3R and repairs were commenced five days later on site by No. 71 Maintenance Unit. Additional repairs were carried out by the manufacturers, which began on 19 September, but to no avail. This work was later abandoned and on 14 January 1975 the aircraft was declared Cat 5. On 30 September 1976 XL384 was allocated as an escape trainer (noted at Scampton, minus its tail fin and rudder, August 1977) until 29 January 1981 when it was then used for crash rescue training (removed from dump 1983, SoC 23 May 1985, scrapped 1994).

A further ex-Blue Steel aircraft arrived on 21 October 1971 in the form of XL359, which remained with the OCU for the next nine-and-a-half years. It was only four days after the arrival of XL359 that the OCU saw the departure of XH563, which made its way to Bitteswell, initially to receive manufacturer's modifications followed by a conversion to equip the aircraft for its future role with No. 27 Sqn. By the end of 1971 the number of Vulcans allocated to the OCU was ten (XH534, XH537, XH538, XH554, XH559, XL359–61, XL386 and XL388).

With 1971 behind it, No. 27 Sqn would only have three months remaining before it was due to disband. Once again more of the 'XL' serial Vulcans with Olympus 201 series engines would become available and were to find their way to the OCU. When No. 27 Sqn reformed in 1973, it was given a different task to perform and its aircraft no longer required the use of Terrain-Following Radar. In 1971 there were five Vulcan B.Mk2s in the RAF that had never been equipped with Terrain-Following Radar and all were operating with No. 230 OCU (XH534, XH537, XH554, XH559 and XH563). Two, XH554 and XH559, remained with the OCU whilst the remaining three were eventually allocated to No. 27 Sqn to carry out the new task. As previously mentioned, XH563 had already been selected for conversion and on 7 April 1972 XH534 left the OCU to be converted in the same manor, but only after a year in storage. As an initial replacement for XH534 the OCU received XL389 on the same day (7 April) and it remained with it for just under three months before being returned to No. 617 Sqn on 30 June. Coincidentally this aircraft was with

Figure 1.9:
XH554 of No. 230 OCU seen during a display sequence at Squires Gate on 5 May 1972 (notice the air brakes above the wing).
(John Huggon)

the OCU when it originally entered service in 1962. On 14 January 1972 XH537 began to receive further manufacturer's modifications, which took until 17 June to complete, before being returned to the OCU. XL388 also received manufacturer's modifications, which began on 28 January 1972 and were completed on 24 May.

On 29 March 1972 No. 27 Sqn disbanded as a bomber squadron and on that day two of its aircraft, XL320 and XL321, joined the OCU. Just under two months later on 18 May, XL361 was involved in a ground accident, but it returned to service after receiving repairs. This is in contrast to the incident that occurred in November 1981, when the same aircraft was involved in a further ground accident (see Chapter IX).

On 22 May 1972 the OCU received XL318, which had previously been part of the Scampton Wing. From 5 July to 9 August the OCU on a number of occasions operated XL387 of No. 617 Sqn before the aircraft was officially transferred to the OCU on 10 August 1972. From 19 July 1972 to 5 December 1973, XL444 of No. 617 Sqn is shown as being shared with the OCU. Two more ex-Blue Steel Vulcans, XL426 and XL427, were used by the OCU during 1972, with XL426 swapping between No. 617 Sqn and No. 230 OCU on several occasions, for about one month at a time (29 March–7 April, 28 June–4 July, 11 July–1 August 1972 and 13–16 April 1973). XL427 initially operated with the OCU for a week (29 June–5 July) before joining on 25 September 1972.

By September some of the aircraft began to display the Unit's insignia on the tail fin once again. XL386 was seen at the Battle of Britain Open Day at Leuchars on 16 September displaying the new markings depicting a golden sword on a blue wave background, placed inside a white circle. Also seen by the public on the same day, but at the Open Day at Wattisham, was XL320. Three days later XL319 returned to Scampton to serve once again with the OCU, having just received its manufacturer's

Figure 1.10:
Vulcan B.Mk2 XL388 flown by a No. 230 OCU crew (Capt Flt Lt Alan Chapman; Co-Pilot Flt Lt Dave Thomas) in formation with VC 10 XV103 (Capt, Sdn Ldr Yates) on 14 August 1972 to publicize the amalgamation of Bomber and Transport Commands to form Strike Command. **(Crown Copyright/ MOD)**

Craig Bulman

modifications at Woodford (8 May–19 September 1972). Also during the same month XL388 was loaned to No. 617 Sqn (15–29 September). In October both XL318 and XL320 left the OCU to receive further modifications (17 October 1972–4 April 1973 and 20 October 1972–22 February 1973 respectively, XL318 is understood to have received a major service at St Athan, beginning 2 August). On 22 November 1972, XL359 was returned to the OCU after the completion of its manufacturer's modifications, which originally commenced on 3 July 1972.

Over the previous two years a lot of ex-Blue Steel aircraft had passed through the OCU for varying periods, but by the summer of 1973 the resident Vulcans on the Unit began to settle down. The Vulcans currently on strength at the end of 1972 were: XH538, XH554, XH559, XL319, XL321, XL359–61, XL386–8, XL427 and XL444 (as mentioned XL444 was used by No. 617 Sqn and the OCU, July 1972–December 1973). This very high allocation of aircraft clearly corresponds with the period that No. 27 Sqn was out of action, when there would have been a further surplus of aircraft.

At the beginning of 1973 XL387 transferred a few miles south to join the Waddington Wing (10 January 1973). By this point more Vulcans had their national markings toned down, as the red and blue paint was extended over the white. The undersides of the aircraft were then painted light aircraft grey, although the rear of the radome remained white (sometimes referred to as a 'bib'). XL387 was one of the earlier Vulcans to be seen with the bib and the low-visibility markings. Another aircraft of the OCU, XL388, also displayed this colour scheme and was initially transferred to No. 617 Sqn from 2 February to 14 May before officially joining it on 1 November 1973. On 1 April 1974 the aircraft was then transferred to the Waddington Wing. Back in January 1973 the OCU loaned two of No. 617 Sqn's Vulcans for a few days (XL389 from the 12th to the 16th and XL392, 12th–15th).

On 1 November 1973 No. 27 Sqn reformed at Scampton to carry out operational sorties of a different kind. It would take time before enough appropriately equipped Vulcans became available, but in the meantime the squadron made use of some standard B.Mk2s. On 3 December 1973 XH538 transferred from the OCU to the newly reformed squadron, although it continued to be used by the OCU on a number of occasions from 9 January to 8 March 1974.

One of the longest serving Vulcans on the OCU (XH554) was involved in a Cat 3R flying accident on 13 September 1973. However, after receiving the necessary repairs it returned to service and continued to train further aircrew. At the end of 1973 the Vulcans allocated to the OCU were: XH554, XH559, XL318–21, XL359–61, XL386 and XL427. Another of the Unit's aircraft, XH537, had yet to return to service as it was still receiving manufacturer's modifications.

Seven of these aircraft (XL318–21 and XL359–61) had already served alongside one another when they first entered service with No. 617 Sqn during 1961/62 in the Blue Steel role. The eighth aircraft that served with the previous seven at that time was XL317, which remained with No. 617 Sqn throughout its service, although it is recorded as being used by No. 230 OCU for one week in 1974 (24 April–1 May). On 4 January 1974 XL427 followed in the footsteps of XH538 by transferring to No. 27 Sqn. During 1974 the crews of No. 27 Sqn made frequent use of XL361, which was used to fly a number of the squadron's sorties. Two other Vulcans were loaned to the OCU during that year from No. 617 Sqn (XL388 on 5 March and XL390 31 May–4 June). For a day only on 3 May 1974, XL319 was loaned to No. 617 Sqn.

On 5 March 1974 XL386 left Scampton to receive further manufacturer's modifications, which took until 21 October 1974 to complete before returning to the OCU. In the absence of XL386, No. 617 Sqn loaned XL388 (5 May), XL390 (31 May–4 June) and the previously mentioned XL317 to the OCU. During the second half of December, XL361 was loaned to the MoD Procurement Executive at the A&AEE (16 December–10 January 1975). This aircraft was then returned to the OCU for four days before being allocated to No. 617 Sqn.

On 15 January 1975 XH538 returned to the OCU from No. 27 Sqn. The vacancy it created was filled by XM571 returning to the UK from the NEAF in Cyprus. At this time Nos 9 and 35 Sqns were about to be relocated to the UK owing to the Turkish invasion of the northern side of the island in 1974.

Two of the Conversion Unit's Vulcans, XL318 and XL360, served with the Waddington Wing for two months at a time during 1975 in order to maintain numbers with the four resident squadrons (18 June–5 August and 18 August–21 October respectively). At the end of 1975 the following eleven Vulcans were allocated to the OCU: XH537, XH538, XH554, XH559, XL318–21, XL359, XL360 and XL386.

Having been back with the OCU for just over a year, XH538 was flown to the manufacturers to receive modifications commencing 9 February 1976. On completion of this work (28 July 1977), the aircraft returned to service and was allocated to No. 35 Sqn. On 8 June 1976 XL321 was flown to Waddington and by the July No. 44 Sqn's insignia had been applied to its tail fin. This aircraft remained with the squadron until 8 November 1976, before returning to Scampton to rejoin the OCU.

For ten days in October 1976 (19th–29th), XM602 of No. 9 Sqn (Olympus 301 series engines) is shown as been loaned to the OCU. Also shown as being temporarily attached to the OCU from 18 October to 29 November 1976 is XH558 (B.Mk2 MRR) and XL427 from 11 to 22 August 1976 (both belonging to No. 27 Sqn). At the end of the year the individual aircraft allocated to the OCU remained the same as the previous year, with the exception of XH538.

Fifty-five days into 1977 (24 February) saw the departure of XL360 from the OCU to receive manufacturer's modifications. When this aircraft returned to service (5 December 1977) it was allocated to No. 617 Sqn for six months before transferring to No. 35 Sqn at the end of May 1978. Ten days prior to XL360 leaving, the OCU saw the arrival onto the Unit of XJ824, coming from No. 35 Sqn. This aircraft would now remain with the Conversion Unit until October 1979.

On 27 September 1977 XH562 of No. 44 Sqn had just completed its major service at St Athan, after which it was delivered to the OCU. Three days later XL386 transferred to the Waddington Wing and by March 1978 it was displaying the markings of No. 44 Sqn. The only other aircraft shown as being attached to the OCU during 1977 was XM570 of No. 35 Sqn (28 February–2 March). By the end of 1977 the aircraft allocated to the OCU were: XH537, XH554, XH559, XH562, XJ824, XL318–21 and XL359.

At RAF Finningley in Yorkshire at the end of July 1977 all of the squadrons within the RAF placed an aircraft on static display bearing the appropriate Unit's insignia to mark the Queens Jubilee Year. All of the Vulcans on display appeared to be in pristine condition, possibly with freshly painted camouflage and markings. XH559, which lacks the Terrain-Following Radar, is shown to have operated with the OCU throughout 1977, but was seen at the event representing No. 35 Sqn.

On 14 February 1978 XH537 left the OCU to begin a conversion, equipping it for the appropriate operations with No. 27 Sqn. This conversion

Figure 1.11:
XL359 displaying the OCU's insignia on its tail fin whilst at Waddington in August 1977. Notice that the aircraft has not yet received the passive ECM tail fin, in contrast to XJ782 of No. 27 Sqn in the background.
(Author's collection)

Figure 1.12:
Display crew of No. 230 OCU, RAF Scampton in 1978 (all QFIs), Barry Mullen (Nav Radar), Dave McGee (Nav Plotter), Fred Tiernan (Capt), Paul Millikin (Co-Pilot) and John Hathaway (AEO). The flying displays conducted by this team during 1978 were: RAF Henlow (25 May, XL318), Bergstrom AFB Austin, Texas (5 August, XL321) and Aufdemdumpel, Germany (2 September, XL359). **(CBV)**

took less than three months in contrast to XH534 (twelve months), XH558 (thirteen months), XH560 (thirteen months) and XH563 (eight months). This was probably due to the fact that XH537 (ex-Skybolt trials' aircraft) already had the necessary wing strengthening required for the carriage of the pods and pylons, which No. 27 Sqn was now using in its new role.

From 6 March to the end of May 1978 XL319 received a major service at St Athan. This aircraft was then returned to the OCU for five months before being transferred to No. 35 Sqn at Scampton on 16 October. On the same day (16 October) XL445 of No. 35 Sqn made the reverse journey to join the OCU.

Towards the end of the year (18 December 1978) RAF St Athan in Wales completed the five hundredth Vulcan major service on XM573 of No. 44 Sqn. This Vulcan is recorded as joining the OCU at that point in time and remaining with it until 7 April 1981. Although in June 1979 XM573 was on display to the public at the annual Waddington Open Day displaying No. 44 Sqn's insignia on its tail fin, this aircraft is known to have transferred to the OCU by 14 August 1979.

From 2 March–21 December 1979 XL445 was at Bitteswell receiving manufacturer's modifications. Meanwhile No. 44 Sqn at Waddington took charge of XJ824 in October 1979, whilst the Waddington Wing was loaned XL318 from 7 November 1979–21 February 1980 before returning it to the OCU. By the end of December 1979 the following eight aircraft were operating with the OCU: XH554, XH559, XH562, XL320, XL321, XL359, XL445 and XM573.

(See colour Plate 1)

During 1980 a number of Vulcans throughout the force began to receive the wrap-round camouflage scheme, consisting of dark green and dark sea grey. Three of the OCU's aircraft were painted in the new colour scheme whilst at RAF St Athan undergoing major servicing (XL318 17 July–7 October, XL359 by May 1980 and XL445 by March 1981).

On 15 February 1980 XH562 arrived at Bitteswell for manufacturer's modifications, where it remained until 16 December 1980. When this aircraft returned to service it was allocated to No. 35 Sqn at Scampton. At that point there were only eight months remaining before the OCU would disband, becoming the first Unit to do so in the run down of the Vulcan Force.

At the beginning of 1981 the following aircraft — XH554, XH559, XL318, XL320, XL321, XL359, XL445 and XM573 — were still allocated to the OCU to continue training further aircrew for the Vulcan Force. On 18 February 1981 it was one of the Vulcans operating with the OCU that flew the 500,000th Vulcan hour — the aircraft that had the honour was XL320.

Pending disbandment in the near future, plans were being made to relocate and dispose of the individual aircraft. The first of these Vulcans to leave the OCU was XM573, which is shown as rejoining the Waddington Wing on 7 April 1981 before being allocated to No. 9 Sqn the following month. The second to go was XH559, which flew to St Athan on 27 May 1981. After arriving at its destination, XH559 ended up with the distinction of having the most flying hours on its airframe (7,313.15 hrs). This aircraft was initially declared Cat 5C (salvage of useful components) before being placed on the dump and eventually scrapped in January 1982. In June 1981 two more of the Unit's aircraft were disposed of, with XL320 going to St Athan (Cat 5C) on the 6th (scrapped in August 1981) and XH554 flying to Catterick for the Fire Fighting Training School on 9 June 1981. XH554 had flown 6,740 hrs, of which the vast majority

Figure 1.13:
Photographed whilst practising an emergency approach and overshoot at Teesside Airport (ex-RAF Middleton St George, V-Bomber dispersal airfield) is XH562 on 22 March 1979 at 17:05 hours. Note the twin blisters on the port wing. (CBV)

was spent training aircrew to equip the frontline squadrons, in which it once played a role (No. 83 Sqn 1961/62). XH554 was eventually destroyed in February 1984. On 1 July 1981 the remaining four aircraft were all transferred to the two remaining bomber squadrons at Scampton (XL318 to No. 617 Sqn, XL321, XL359 and XL445 to No. 35 Sqn). No. 230 OCU officially disbanded on 31 August 1981.

We should all remember that No. 230 OCU was responsible for training the flight crews that made up the Vulcan Force for over twenty-five years, a role which began with the B.Mk1 at RAF Waddington on 31 May 1956. This Unit played a vital part in the defence of the country and in doing so helped maintain global peace.

Figure 1.14:
Vulcan B.Mk2
XH554 alongside
Shackleton AEW.2
WL745 and Victor
K.1A XH647, all
positioned on RAF
Catterick's dump on
8 May 1982 to be
used by the Fire
Fighting and Safety
School.
(Author's collection)

02

Blue Steel and the Scampton Wing

As early as 1954 it was realized that in order to increase the effectiveness of the RAF's intended new generation of medium bombers it would require a 'stand-off capability'. By releasing a missile from at least one hundred nautical miles from its intended target, the aircraft would not have to penetrate so deep into Soviet airspace.

F ROM THIS CONCEPT A.V. Roe produced the Blue Steel Nuclear Stand Off Weapon. After trials with a two-fifths scale model, flown on Valiant WP204 in 1957, a Vulcan B.Mk1 (XA903) began trials on the full-size Blue Steel by making a number of launches over the Aberporth range in 1958.

Trials continued throughout 1959 from Woodford and then at Woomera in Australia in the summer of 1960, the latter seeing XA903 launch full-scale Blue Steels made of stainless steel and powered by the Stentor rocket motor.

Development continued with two Vulcan B.Mk2s (XH538 and XH539) joining the trials. The production version of Blue Steel was first tested at the Woomera range when XH539 launched the missile in early 1961. XH538 was also used to test a wide range of systems on board the aircraft.

After completion of the trials, XH538 was modified to carry Skybolt and remained with the Ministry of Aviation until 31 May 1965, at which point it entered service with the RAF to serve for the next three years with No. 230 OCU at Finningley. It was subsequently returned to the manufacturers for refit on 12 August 1968, before being issued to the Scampton Wing to serve in the free-fall bombing role on 14 May 1969.

Meanwhile, XH539 continued to serve with the Ministry of Aviation/A&AEE operating from Boscombe Down. The aircraft remained in its white colour scheme during its operational life until 7 March 1972. It was then flown to Waddington to be placed on the dump for crash rescue training where the aircraft was painted all over 'olive drab'. XH539 expired in 1987.

In order to carry Blue Steel some modifications were required including replacing the bomb doors with a new fairing where the missile would sit semi-recessed. To accommodate the upper part of the missile, the rear spar in the bomb bay had a section cut out and a crank was formed in the front spar. The first Vulcan to receive these modifications was the twenty-sixth B.Mk2 off the production line (XL317). This aircraft was also the first Vulcan ordered as a B.Mk2 — all of the previous twenty-five XH and XJ aircraft were originally ordered as B.Mk1s but delivered as B.Mk2s. XL317 first flew in July 1961 and spent the next eleven months with the Ministry of Aviation before being delivered to No. 617 (Dambuster) Sqn at Scampton on 7 June 1962. This was the eighth B.Mk2 to arrive at No. 617 Sqn, as seven other aircraft had been delivered during its absence with the Ministry of Aviation. These were Production Nos 27–33, XL318 (4 September 1961), XL319 (23 October 1961), XL320 (4 December 1961), XL321 (11 January 1962), XL359 (1 February 1962), XL360 (2 March 1962) and XL361 (13 March 1962).

No. 617 Sqn was now fully equipped with the B.Mk2 (all eight fitted with flight-refuelling probes). Its four Mk1s and five Mk1As made the short flight south to Waddington to arm the recently reformed No. 50 Sqn on 1 August 1961. No. 617 Sqn at Scampton became the first to equip with Blue Steel in the late summer of 1962, but not before further modifications had been carried out at station level to each aircraft. By October 1962 an emergency operational capability had been achieved (this was at the time of the Cuban missile crises). The squadron became fully operational in February 1963.

During 1962 two more Vulcan Units, Nos 27 and 83 Sqns operating from Scampton, were to be allocated the Blue Steel missile. No. 83 Sqn had been the first operator of the Vulcan B.Mk1 on 21 May 1957 at Waddington and also the first to equip with the B.Mk2, receiving XH563 at Scampton on 28 December 1960. When the squadron reformed at Scampton it left behind its B.Mk1As at Waddington to form No. 44 Sqn.

No. 83 Sqn received XL392 (equipped with a flight-refuelling probe) as its first Blue Steel Vulcan B.Mk2 on 2 August 1962. This was followed by XL425 on 11 August 1962, XL426 (13 September 1962), XL427 (2 October 1962) and XL443 (8 October 1962). These five aircraft were Production Nos 42–6. At this point in time, four of No. 83 Sqn's earlier XH and XJ B.Mk2s departed Scampton and headed for Coningsby to equip the newly reformed No. 12 Sqn. The Vulcans involved were XH563, XJ780, XJ781 and XJ782 (Production Nos 17–20).

In November No. 83 Sqn's remaining two B.Mk2s from the earlier production batches were also despatched to other Units. XH554 joined No.230 OCU on 1 November 1962 with XJ783 joining No. 9 Sqn at Coningsby on 7 November 1962.

On 14 November 1962 three Vulcan B.Mk2s departed from Scampton embarking on a round-the-world flight (XH556 No. 27 Sqn, XL392 No. 83 Sqn and XL319 No. 617 Sqn). The Vulcans, along with a number of RAAF Sabres, conducted a flypast at Perth, Australia to mark the opening of the 1962 British Empire and Commonwealth Games. Towards the end of the month whilst in Australia, the three Vulcans spent time at RAAF Richmond in Sydney before flying to New Zealand, a visit that coincided with the twentieth anniversary of the RNZAF. The aircraft then returned home to Scampton via the USA. Although the complete trip was spread over a number of weeks, the aircraft completed the full 30,000 miles in fifty hours flying time.

The next five Blue Steel Vulcans delivered from the Woodford production line (Nos 47–51) to join the frontline strength of the RAF were: XL444 arriving at Scampton on 1 November 1962, XL445 (26 November 1962), XL446 (30 November 1962), XM569 (1 February 1963) and XM570 (27 February 1963). The five previously mentioned aircraft were all issued to No. 27 Sqn. This squadron was already operating five earlier XH and XJ (free-fall equipped) Vulcan B.Mk2s out of Scampton. Following the arrival of XL446 in the November, the squadron had eight Vulcans on strength. As a consequence plans were made to exchange the free-fall-equipped Vulcans, pending the delivery from Woodford of further new Blue Steel aircraft. XH555 and XH556 were both transferred to No. 230 OCU across at Finningley in Yorkshire. Meanwhile, in January and February 1963, XJ823–5 made their way south-east to join the Coningsby Wing. Both XJ823 and XJ825 joined No. 35 Sqn on 2 January and 4 February 1963 respectively, whilst No. 9 Sqn took delivery of XJ824 on 25 February 1963.

As more new Vulcans arrived Nos 27 and 83 Sqns were soon to be at full strength having eight aircraft each. Production Nos 52–4 were all issued to No. 83 Sqn beginning with XM571 on 22 February 1963, XM572 (28 February 1963) and XM573 (28 March 1963). The next five Blue Steel-equipped Vulcans to leave Woodford (Production Nos 55–9) were different to all of the previously mentioned aircraft because they were equipped with Olympus 301 series engines. On 21 June 1963, No. 27 Sqn received both XM574 and XM576 followed four weeks later by XM594 on

Figure 2.1:
XM570 of No. 27 Sqn at Le Bourget in France on 15 June 1963 carrying Blue Steel.
(John Huggon)

Figure 2.2:
XM575 of No. 617 Sqn at Le Bourget on 15 June 1963 with Olympus 301 series engines. Note the shorter exhaust pipes on this aircraft compared with those on XM570 in Figure 2.1.
(John Huggon)

Figure 2.3:
Members of No. 2394 East Cleveland Squadron of the Air Training Corps pictured next to XL319 of No. 617 Sqn during their annual camp (Scampton, 17–24 August 1963). On one of the final days of their camp they were instructed to find a vantage point close to the hangars but in view of the runway in order to see all of the station's serviceable Vulcans take-off in quick succession during an exercise. The aircraft's serial number is identifiable on the air intake cover.
(CBV via Ken Thompson)

19 July 1963. This now brought the squadron up to full strength. No. 617 Sqn received the remaining two aircraft with XM575 arriving on 22 May 1963 and XM595 on 21 August 1963.

With the arrival of XM575 at Scampton in May, No. 617 Sqn now had a spare aircraft. This allowed No. 617 Sqn to loan XL361 to the Ministry of Aviation (3–15 July 1963 and 14 August 1963–2 April 1964).

By the end of 1963, Nos 27, 83 and 617 Sqns were each operational with Blue Steel and had a combined strength of twenty-six Vulcan B.Mk2s all operating out of Scampton (XL361 on loan to the Ministry of Aviation). Meanwhile their Blue Steel missiles were systematically being serviced just a short distance away at Faldingworth, No. 92 Maintenance Unit was carrying out this task. The story of the Blue Steel Vulcan B.Mk2s, however, does not end here.

In due course Scampton would receive a further seven Vulcan B.Mk2s with Blue Steel capability. The aircraft involved were XL384–90 (Production Nos 34–40). XL384, XL387 and XL389 were operating at Finningley with No. 230 OCU, whilst XL385, XL386, XL388 and XL390 were stationed at Coningsby with No. 9 Sqn and could be identified either by the large green bat or the squadron badge. These seven aircraft would

Figure 2.4: *Originally XL384 entered service with No. 230 OCU at Finningley equipped with Olympus 201 series engines, but when the aircraft was modified to carry Blue Steel it received 301 series engines (notice the difference in size and shape of the exhaust pipes). In the first photo XL384 is seen at Finningley's Battle of Britain Day on 15 September 1962 displaying the Yorkshire rose on the tail fin, whilst in the second photo it is pictured in the late 1960s (possibly at Scampton, September 1969). (APN)*

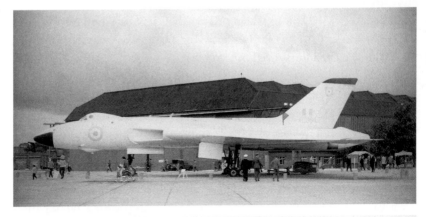

soon return to the manufacturer at Woodford for a retrofit, where improvements would be made to existing radars, jammers and sensors, as well as receiving additional equipment. They would also have their Olympus 201 engines replaced by the more powerful 301 series engines.

In August 1963 XM597, fitted with Olympus 301 series engines and Skybolt attachment points, was about to enter service with No. 12 Sqn at Coningsby replacing XJ780 (201 series), which was to be transferred to No. 230 OCU at Finningley on 16 August 1963. XJ780 then became the replacement for XL384 that flew from Finningley to Woodford on 7 August 1963 and would remain there for the next 12 months.

XL385 arrived back at its birthplace (Woodford) on 1 October 1963 joined by XL386 from Coningsby on 4 November 1963. Subsequently on 5 November 1963, No. 9 Sqn received XM601 as a replacement for the latter aircraft.

The next Vulcan to be returned to the manufacturer was XL387, arriving on 2 December 1963 and at the same time XJ824 of No. 9 Sqn transferred to the OCU. Two days later the vacant slot on No. 9 Sqn was taken by the sixty-seventh production Vulcan XM603. On 30 December 1963 XM605 also joined No. 9 Sqn. This allowed XL388 to depart for Woodford after the new year (2 January 1964). At the end of January XM609 was delivered to No. 12 Sqn, replacing XJ781 that flew to Finningley for the OCU (2 February 1964). On the same day XL389 was released from the OCU and departed for Woodford.

The last of the seven aircraft to be returned to Woodford for a retrofit was XL390 arriving on 2 March 1964. No. 9 Sqn received a replacement the next day in the form of XM612. This was the seventy-sixth production Vulcan B.Mk2 and the last of seventeen fitted with the complete Skybolt attachment points during construction.

The time to complete the retrofit would be between 12 and 15 months. These seven Vulcans would return to service equipped with Blue Steel to substitute aircraft of the Scampton Wing, which would then make the reverse journey to Woodford for their retrofit.

On 2 April 1964, XL361, which had been on loan to the Ministry of Aviation, returned to No. 617 Sqn at Scampton allowing XL318 (No. 617 Sqn's first Vulcan B2) to depart the same day. The process of updating and modernizing the original 26 Blue Steel Vulcans had begun. Also in 1964 the decision was taken to operate the V-Bombers at low level to maintain the effectiveness and 'survivability' of the aircraft against the increasing threat of Soviet surface-to-air missiles. Previous high-level operations would now be deemed vulnerable and ineffective. Low-level activity placed additional stresses on the Vulcans and to compensate for this their airframes received additional strengthening. The manufacturer Avro removed the sixtieth B.Mk2 (XM596) from the production line and subjected it to stress testing in order to obtain vital information about the airframe's weakest points. Hydraulic jacks were placed around XM596's airframe to simulate the stresses applied to the aircraft as if in flight. The remedies required to overcome these weaknesses were then applied to the entire Vulcan fleet. The Vulcans would also have their upper surfaces camouflaged (dark green and medium grey) and in due course would receive Terrain-Following Radar which was placed in a small thimble at the tip of the aircraft's nose. Low-level operations also reduced the range of the Blue Steel missile to about 100 miles. The Vulcan, along with the aircrew, adapted admirably to this different and demanding environment.

The 4 May 1964 saw the arrival of XL319 into Woodford for retrofit. The absence of XL318 and XL319 from the Scampton Wing would mean the remaining number of Blue Steel-equipped Vulcans on strength would have been twenty-four. On 5 August 1964 XL384 returned to service. This Vulcan arrived with a flight-refuelling probe fitted, Olympus 301 series engines, twin flat ECM plates between both pairs of engines and displaying the new green and grey upper surface camouflage. XL385–90 were to arrive with the same modifications.

Seven days after the delivery of XL384 to the Scampton Wing, XL320 departed to Woodford (12 August). The next exchange occurred two months later when XM595 left Scampton on 8 October requiring fewer modifications and taking only four months. The very next day XL385 made the reverse journey when it re-entered service. The next Vulcan to return to the manufacturers was XM575 (11 November 1964), requiring similar modifications to that of XM595. The Scampton Wing's strength would now have been twenty-three Vulcan B.Mk2s.

Within two days of XL386 re-entering squadron service (7 December 1964), XL359 returned home to Woodford (9 December 1964). In the new year (4 January 1965) XM576 departed to receive the same modifications as XM575 and XM595. The Scampton Wing would now have had twenty-two aircraft. In February 1965,

Figure 2.5:
Thundering past is XL446 of the Scampton Wing seen during its display at Acklington on 19 September 1964. With close inspection of the port ECM plate, it is possible to see the two additional wedge-shaped blisters (ECM aerials). These two additional aerials only appear on some of the Vulcans equipped with Blue Steel.
(John Huggon)

XM595, XL387 and XL388 made their way to Scampton arriving on the 4th, 5th and 22nd respectively. Heading in the opposite direction during the same month were XL360 on the 1st and XL317 on the 18th. In March both XM575 and XM576 returned to Scampton on 22nd and 29th respectively. It was at this point that the remaining two Vulcans of the original eight issued to No. 617 Sqn flew to Woodford for their retrofit (XL321, 12 March–21 December 1965 and XL361, 25 March 1965–20 January 1966). All eight Vulcans (Production Nos 26–33, XL317–21 and XL359–61) had now been taken out of service and were simultaneously positioned back inside Avro's facilities.

No. 83 Sqn's first Blue Steel Vulcan (XL392) made the flight to Woodford on 1 April 1965 and returned to service after completion of the retrofit on 23 February 1966. XL318 returned to service at Scampton on 21 April 1965. Centralized servicing, which was introduced in March 1963, meant that squadrons no longer had ownership of individual aircraft and instead would draw from the Scampton Wing's allocation of Vulcans on a day-to-day basis. As a result of this, individual squadron markings on both the tail and fuselage were removed and reapplied in miniature to the crew entrance door, together with the station badge (changed in 1958 pending the arrival of the Vulcan Bombers), which depicted a 'Bow and Arrow' set at forty-five degrees. The bowstring on the badge represents the original Ermine Street (A15), whilst the bow indicates the new bend in the A15 road to accommodate the runway extension and the arrow represents the 9000-ft runway.

On 29 March 1965 XM576 re-entered service, but this was to be short lived. Only fifty-eight days later (25 May 1965) the aircraft was written-off after attempting to land on a practice asymmetric approach to RAF Scampton's main runway. XM576 crash landed and came to rest on its belly on the south side of the runway close to the air traffic control building. The cause of the crash was due to the fact that the two port engines, which had been throttled back to idle during the approach, failed to respond immediately when full throttle was reapplied to all four engines in order to overshoot. The starboard engines, which were at a higher operating temperature, responded instantly as they had been in constant use during the flight. As a result, the aircraft swung sharply to the left, the wing-tip struck the ground, the port

Figure 2.6: Having initially entered service with the Coningsby Wing in 1962, allowing No. 9 Sqn to increase its strength, XL390 later (in 1964) received a retrofit and conversion to equip it for Blue Steel operations. The aircraft is photographed during a display at Acklington (North East of England) on 18 September 1965. (John Huggon)

undercarriage broke away, the nose wheel leg came adrift and the aircraft came to rest.

During the latter part of May 1965 both XL389 and XL390 returned to service on 20th and 27th respectively. This meant that the additional seven B.Mk2s, earmarked for the Scampton Wing after completion of a retro-fit, had finally joined the frontline as part of Britain's Nuclear Deterrent Force equipped with Blue Steel.

Between May and October five more Vulcans were stood down to receive a retrofit in exchange for five returning to service. The aircraft involved being XL425 (14 May 1965–2 March 1966), XL426 (21 June 1965–11 March 1966), XL427 (13 August 1965–13 April 1966) and XL443 (7 September 1965–approx. May 1966). These four Vulcans were all from the initial batch of Blue Steel aircraft delivered to No. 83 Sqn three years previously. The fifth Vulcan to be stood down was XL444 from 13 September 1965 to 3 May 1966. The aircraft had originally been No. 27 Sqn's first Blue Steel-equipped Vulcan. The five aircraft returning to rejoin the Scampton Wing were all ex-No. 617 Sqn aircraft: XL319 on 22 July 1965 followed by XL359 (3 September 1965), XL320 (30 September 1965), XL360 (19 October 1965) and XL317 (29 October 1965).

All in all the Scampton Wing had operated thirty-three Blue Steel-equipped Vulcan B.Mk2s to date (Production Nos 26–59, with the exception of XL391, Production No. 41). XL391 did not enter frontline service until July 1968 when it joined the Cottersmore Wing. Previously the air-craft was involved in numerous trials with the Ministry of Aviation, A&AEE and the Bomber Command Development Unit. It had been fit-ted with the full Skybolt attachment points and 301 series engines from the start. These additional features delayed its completion on the produc-tion line until 22 May 1963, just three months before the first of the similar equipped Vulcans entered service (XM597 26 August 1963). XL391 was still in service at RAF Waddington in April 1982 with No. 101 Sqn at the time of the Falkland's crisis. It was because of the previously men-tioned fitting of the Skybolt attachment points that XL391 had been selected as a reserve aircraft for the Black Buck raids, but it remained at Waddington during the Falkland's War as it lacked certain pieces of equipment that the four main Black Buck Vulcans possessed.

By the end of October 1965 twenty-four of the thirty-three Blue Steel Vulcans had been involved in the retrofit programme. This left only nine aircraft waiting their turn. Seven of these Vulcans were fitted with 201 series engines (XL445, XL446, XM569–73) and the remaining two having 301 series engines (XM574 and XM594). Owing to the fact that the seven additional B.Mk2s (XL384–90) were all now in service, the remaining 201 series Vulcans were surplus to requirement in the Blue Steel role. After their appropriate retrofit, the seven 201 series Vulcans were, in the main, issued to the Waddington Wing to replace the B.Mk1As. XM571 was issued to the Cottersmore Wing to cover for aircraft that were out of service for manufacturer's modifications. XL446 and XM569 initially returned to the Scampton Wing after retrofits for a short spell, then headed south to Waddington. XM572 is shown as returning to the Scampton Wing for over a year, but it joined the Waddington Wing on 8 February 1967. These seven 201 series Vulcans eventually all served with the Near East Air Force Bomber Wing at Akrotiri in Cyprus after transferring to Cottersmore from Waddington. The appropriate dates for the retrofits were XL445 from 22 November 1965–30 September 1966, XL446 (18 October 1965– 18 June 1966), XM569 (16 December 1965–29 August 1966), XM570 (13 January 1966–2 January 1967), XM571 (22 February 1966–20 January 1967), XM572 (28 February 1966–8 January 1967) and XM573 (11 March 1966–25 April 1967). The remaining two 301 series Vulcans received similar modifications to XM575 and XM595 where less time was required. The dates for these aircraft were: XM594, 30 December 1965–16 May 1966; and XM574, 28 January–13 June 1966. Both Vulcans returned to the Scampton Wing.

On 6 April 1967 the Scampton Wing suffered a second loss of a Blue Steel Vulcan. XL385 had taxied and lined up on runway 05 at its home base with five aircrew and a sixteen-year-old air cadet on board. The aircraft was carrying a Blue Steel Training Round when numbers 1 and 2 engines exploded. XL385 was completely destroyed by fire but fortunately the crew and passenger escaped. This left the Scampton Wing with twenty-three Vulcans, thirteen 201 series (XL317–21, XL359–61, XL392,

Figure 2.7:
XL443 of the Scampton Wing at Finningley on 17 September 1966.
(John Hemingbrough)

Figure 2.8:
*XM594 at Boscombe
Down in 1967 giving
a display to NATO
officers whilst carry-
ing a Blue Steel
missile. Notice the
dark panel behind
the port under-
carriage indicating
the location of the
Doppler radar and
the single 'coolant'
blister outboard of
the main under-
carriage door. (APN)*

XL425–7 and XL443) and ten 301 series (XL384, XL386–90, XM574, XM575, XM594 and XM595). XL444 had been across at Finningly serving with the OCU for nearly a year (18 June 1966–19 June 1967). The aircraft initially returned to Scampton for four days before being despatched to the manufacturers to receive modifications (23 June–10 August 1967). XL444 then rejoined the Scampton Wing, increasing the number to twenty-four.

Originally Blue Steel was intended to be a preliminary weapon for the V-Force until the planned entry into service of the main weapon, the American-designed Skybolt missile, in 1965–66. However, on 31 December 1962 Prime Minister Harold Macmillan communicated the cancellation of Skybolt, President John F. Kennedy having officially can-celled the missile in November. The intended replacement for Skybolt was to be the Polaris missile. It was to equip and would be launched from Royal Navy submarines. The intended date for introduction into service was about 1970.

The onus now returned to Blue Steel as the main weapon system for the foreseeable future. Blue Steel required upgrading to allow it to oper-ate from both low and high level. Out of the stockpile of fifty-seven Blue Steel missiles shared by Scampton's Vulcans (Nos 27, 83 and 617 Sqns) and Wittering's Victors (Nos 100 and 139 Sqns) four rounds were used for proof firing. Two of the missiles were launched in Operation Fresno, the first of which was launched from a Victor, XH673 of No. 100 Sqn, on

(See colour Plate 2) 27 May 1966. The second launch took place on 26 August 1966 from a

Victor, XH675, of No. 139 Sqn. The first post-acceptance launch from a Vulcan was made on 31 May 1967 from XL390 with a No. 27 Sqn crew on board. A No. 617 Sqn crew carried out the second launch from XL390 on 7 July 1967. All four of the missiles were launched over the Aberporth range and achieved an average impact error of about 800 yards.

During the operational life of Blue Steel, each aircrew was allocated specific targets in the event of war. The aircrews would spend a great deal of time each week familiarizing themselves with their predetermined routes to the intended targets, recognizing roads, rivers, landmarks, etc. A further aspect of training was navigation and on this subject the Scampton Wing actually had an advantage over all of the others, the reason being was that it could 'fly the missile'. The aircrew would fly its sorties by following the information provided by the Blue Steel missile. Before departing Scampton the navigator would input the appropriate coordinates into the missile's 'gyros'. This would then provide the crew with the exact location, i.e. longitude and latitude. At intervals through-out the flight the navigator would update the information given to the missile by taking radar fixes from known landmarks and in return he was provided with the current longitude and latitude.

Throughout the early years of Blue Steel operations, aircraft were held on quick-reaction alert with unarmed and unfuelled missiles fitted to them. The level of safety was perceived to be far too low to allow the volatile fuel, nuclear materials and thermal batteries remaining in close proximity for long periods during peacetime. Over the future years new methods were developed to reduce the time needed to make the missiles serviceable (about ten minutes).

Midnight 30 June 1969 had been earmarked for the exchange of responsibility for the UK Strategic Nuclear Deterrent Force from the RAF to the Royal Navy. During the latter part of 1968, the two Wittering

Figure 2.9: XL320 of the Scampton Wing became the first V-Bomber to land at Kia Tak, Hong Kong. The aircraft is seen upon arrival on 17 April 1969. **(CBV via Rod Powell)**

Figure 2.10:
The Station Commander of Kia Tak (right) welcomes the crew of XL320 shortly after their arrival. The No. 83 Sqn crew is, from left to right: Flt Lt Adrian Lambourne (Capt), two crew chiefs (unknown), Flt Lt Wilbraham (Nav Radar), Fg Off Rod Powell (AEO), Fg Off R. Thomas (Co-Pilot) and Sqn Ldr W. A. (Wally) Mears (Nav Plotter). Notice the recess in the bomb bay for the Blue Steel missile.
(Crown Copyright/ MOD)

squadrons operating Victors (Nos 100 and 139 Sqns) were disbanded as Blue Steel was slowly phased out. The first Vulcan squadron to disband was No. 83 Sqn on 31 August 1969. No. 27 Sqn was to relinquish Blue Steel in the near future and convert to free-fall nuclear/conventional bombing role to become operational by 1 January 1970. In order for the first aircrews of No. 27 Sqn to begin training in their new role, XH538 (ex-Skybolt trials aircraft/ex-OCU) was allocated to the Scampton Wing on 14 May 1969, having just received a retrofit that began on 12 August 1968. This aircraft received further modifications from 27 June to 20 August 1969 before rejoining the Scampton Wing.

Over two years all of the Blue Steel Vulcans would be sent to Hawker Siddeley at either Woodford or Bitteswell for the necessary manufacturer's modifications to return them to free-fall bombing. Each aircraft would be away for two to five months before returning to service.

The process began on 12 August 1969 with XM575; nineteen days before No. 83 squadron was due to disband. This was only forty-three days after the Royal Navy took over the nuclear responsibility. This aircraft returned to Scampton approximately two months later on 21 October 1969. On 27 August 1969, just four days before No. 83 squadron disbanded, XL386 departed to Bitterswell for reconversion and was then returned to service on 31 October 1969. The next four aircraft involved were XL318 on 9 September–18 November 1969, XL320 (30 September–25 November 1969), XL361 (14 October–8 December 1969) and XL426 (28 October–18 December 1969). It would have been in these six Vulcans that the crews of No. 27 squadron trained to become

operational in the new year. Three more Vulcans relinquished their Blue Steel capability when they left the Scampton Wing towards the end of the year and returned a few months later. These were XM595 on 11 November 1969–14 January 1970, XM574 (2 December 1969–30 January 1970) and XL390 (16 December 1969–17 April 1970). During January 1970 four further Vulcans — XL389, XL319, XL425 and XL359 — began to receive the necessary modifications before being returned to the Scampton Wing (7 January–13 May, 12 January–28 April, 12 January–23 March and 23 January–21 May respectively).

No. 617 squadron continued alone, operating the Blue Steel out of Scampton until its final sortie on 21 December 1970. On 2 February 1970 it was the turn of XL384 to revert to conventional bombing. When this aircraft returned to service on 5 June 1970 it was allocated to the Waddington Wing before heading back to Scampton on 27 November 1970 to join No. 230 OCU. XL384 served with the OCU for just over eight months until 12 August 1971, when the aircraft made a heavy landing at Scampton. Initially the aircraft was assessed as Cat 3R (repairable by the RAF Maintenance Unit), but this was later changed to Cat 5 (written off). However, XL384 was resurrected and used as an escape/crash rescue

Figure 2.11:
Informal photograph of No. 83 Sqn standing in front of XL443, under the command of Wg Cdr John Pack, after the presentation of the Medium Bomber Efficiency Trophy on 21 May 1969. Ironically after being declared the most efficient medium bomber squadron by becoming the winners of the trophy, No. 83 Sqn was disbanded three months later (31 August 1969).
(CBV via Rod Powell)

Figure 2.12: *During June 1969, a No. 83 Sqn crew flew XL427 to Akritiri, Cyprus to conduct trials over the Libyan desert of the Auxiliary AVS (Air Ventilation Suit). The team seen in the picture are, from left to right: Dr Allen (RAE Farnborough), Fg Off Russ Oxley (Co-Pilot), Mike Davidson (Nav Plotter), Fg Off Rod Powell (AEO), Flt Lt Neil McDougall (Capt), Flt Lt Morrison (Engineering Off), Flt Lt Graham Morris (Nav Radar), Roger Howells (Engineering Off) and two unknown ground crew seen kneeling. McDougall continued with the Vulcan Force throughout the 1970s and in 1982 he was Captain of XM597 on two of the Black Buck raids during the Falkland's Campaign. Notice the station badge together with the three resident squadrons on the crew entrance door that formed the Scampton Wing.* (**CBV via Rod Powell**)

trainer at Scampton before ending its days on the station's fire dump and scrapped in 1994. Pictures of this Vulcan appear in numerous books and publications where it is shown during its better days over flying Niagara Falls whilst carrying a Blue Steel training round.

Throughout the latter part of 1969, until conversion to free-fall bombing at the end of 1970, No. 617 Sqn's aircraft displayed the three red (dayglow) lightening flashes on the tail fin. On 20 September 1969, four of No. 617 Sqn's Vulcans appeared at the Battle of Britain Open Day at RAF Finningley on the operational readiness platforms angled into the side of the runway. The four aircraft involved were XL321, XL360, XL390 and XL427. On 13 April 1970 the necessary remodification work began on XM594 before returning to service at Scampton on 14 July 1970. Over the summer three further Vulcans began to receive the modifications: XL388 on 18 May–27 June 1970, XL392 (25 June–13 November 1970) and XL444 (27 August–31 December 1970). During the second half of 1970 XM575 served with the Waddington Wing (28 July–27 November 1970) before returning to Scampton. By the end of the year XL319, XL361, XL384 and XL386 had all transferred to No. 230 OCU, which was now based at Scampton instead of Finningley. At the time that No. 617 Sqn conducted its final Blue Steel sortie there were only six Vulcans (XL317, XL321, XL360, XL443, XL387 and XL427) remaining with this missile capability. In the new year the manufacturers began the necessary modification work on two more of the Vulcans (XL317, 21 January–28 May 1971 and XL360, 7 January–12 May 1971). Also during January XL321 was allocated to No. 27 Sqn where the appropriate insignia was applied to the tail fin. This aircraft operated with No. 27 Sqn until March 1972 apart from visiting the manufacturer's facilities to receive modifications between 8 April and 19 August 1971. When the work was completed XL321 was returned to No. 27 Sqn. After receiving modifications (4 March–7 July 1971) XL443 returned to the Scampton Wing for approximately nine months (No. 27 Sqn) before it took up a new posting in Cyprus with the NEAF (Nos 9 and 35 Sqns). The next Blue Steel Vulcan to be reconverted was XL387 (13 May 1971–21 September 1971). This aircraft appeared at the RAF Benson Open Day in September 1970 complete with No. 617 Sqn's day-glow markings, Terrain-Following Radar and Blue Steel. The last remaining Vulcan with Blue Steel capability would therefore have been XL427 (modifications, 17 June–10 November 1971). This aircraft had entered service with No. 83 Sqn on 2 October 1962 and was stationed at Scampton for eight-and-a-half years whilst operating in the Blue Steel role. During that time XL427 had flown around the world and had been photographed in numerous countries. Prior to receiving the modifications the aircraft was transferred to No. 27 Sqn in March 1971. After the work was completed to convert the aircraft back to the free-fall bombing role (10 November 1971) it was returned to No. 27 Sqn until 29 March 1972, at which time it transferred to No. 230 OCU. XL427 was one of the first Vulcans to be noted with the new low-visibility red/blue roundels, whilst at the same time displaying the OCU markings on the tail fin. Apart from a two-month attachment to No. 617 Sqn in the summer of 1972, it remained with the OCU until joining the newly reformed No. 27 Sqn as a standard B.Mk2 on 4 January 1974. In May 1977 the aircraft transferred to the Waddington Wing were it received No. 9 Sqn's insignia the following month. The aircraft retained its high-gloss paint scheme until it received the wrap-round camouflage during its last major service in the

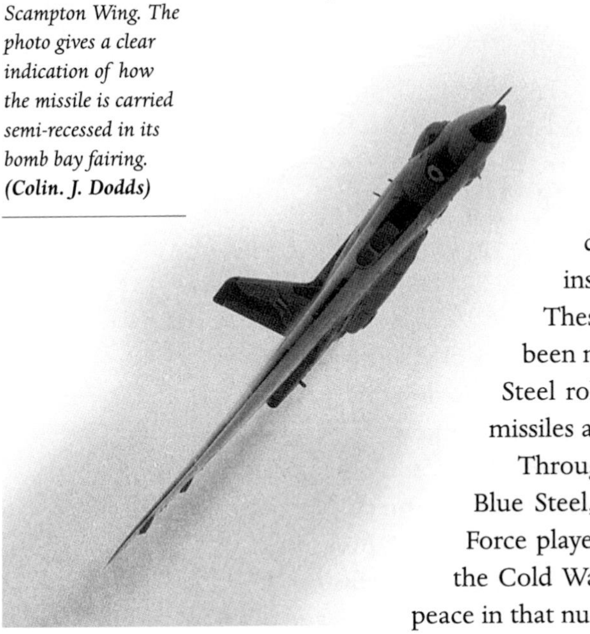

Figure 2.13:
*Seen during a
display (understood
to be possibly Biggin
Hill in 1969/70) is
XL443 of the
Scampton Wing. The
photo gives a clear
indication of how
the missile is carried
semi-recessed in its
bomb bay fairing.*
(Colin. J. Dodds)

early 1980s. It was then seen operating with and displaying the markings of Nos 50, 9 and 44 Sqns during its final years of service, before making its last flight to Macrihanish in Scotland on 13 August 1982 were it was sadly placed on the fire dump after flying 6,133.30 hrs.

One aspect of Blue Steel's existence in the Vulcan Force continued in service long after the missiles themselves were withdrawn. This was the saddle-shaped fuel tank placed in the forward part of the bomb bay. These fuel tanks would have been seen by the public during flying displays and can still be seen today inside a number of Vulcans in museums. These saddle-shaped fuel tanks have also been noted in Vulcans never used in the Blue Steel role. Several examples of the Blue Steel missiles are still on display in some museums.

Throughout the operational service life of Blue Steel, the air- and ground crews of the V-Force played an extremely important part during the Cold War years by helping to maintain global peace in that nuclear era.

03

The Coningsby Wing

By February 1962 Nos 83, 27 and 617 Sqns at RAF Scampton were equipped with the Vulcan B.Mk2. This now meant that the next batch of new Vulcan B.Mk2s coming from the Woodford production line would be available to equip a further squadron. The next squadron selected to reform on the Vulcan Bomber would be No. 9 Sqn (ex-Canberra Unit, RAF Binbrook). No. 9 Sqn would reform at RAF Coningsby, Lincolnshire in March 1962, followed by two further squadrons, Nos 12 and 35 (ex-Canberra Units). Together these three squadrons would form the Coningsby Wing.

WITH MORE SQUADRONS FORMING, No. 230 OCU would also require additional Vulcan B.Mk2s to train the extra crews. In March 1962 the OCU at Finningley had only four B.Mk2s on strength: XH558, XH559, XH561 and XH562. The OCU had also operated a fifth Vulcan B.Mk2 prior to this date in the form of XH560 (3 October–11 November 1960). This aircraft then went back to the manufacturers and after a while transferred to the Ministry of Aviation for trials due to problems with the 201 series engines (13 January 1961). Eighteen days after No. 617 Sqn received XL361 (Production No. 33), No. 230 OCU took delivery of XL384 (Production No. 34), taking its total to five.

Although No. 9 Sqn reformed at Coningsby on 12 March 1962, the squadron did not receive its first Vulcan B.Mk2 for a further five weeks. XL385 (Production No. 35), fitted with Olympus 201 engines, was delivered to No. 9 Sqn on 18 April 1962. The next Vulcan to leave the production line was also delivered to No. 9 Sqn (XL386, 14 May 1962). The squadron took delivery of two more Vulcans: XL388 (14 June 1962) and XL390 (20 July 1962). The OCU at Finningley received XL387 (4 June 1962) and XL389 (13 July 1962), bringing its total to seven B.Mk2s. At this point No. 9 Sqn had four aircraft, all of which were fitted with Olympus 201 series engines.

The second squadron to form at Coningsby was No. 12 on 1 July 1962. The squadron's first Vulcan B.Mk2 XH560 did not arrive until 25 September 1962. After serving with the OCU and then the Ministry of Aviation, this previously mentioned aircraft received manufacturer's modifications (16 March–September 1962) prior to delivery to No. 12 Sqn. XH560 displayed the squadron's 'fox' insignia on its tail fin.

As more new Vulcans came off the production line to equip No. 83 Sqn at Scampton, to operate in the Blue Steel role (XL392, XL425, XL426, XL427 and XL443; Production Nos 42–6), four of No. 83 Sqn's earlier B.Mk2s moved to the south-east of Lincolnshire to equip No. 12 Sqn at Coningsby, XJ782 (23 October 1962), XJ781 (29 October 1962), XH563 and XJ780, both arriving (26 November 1962). Prior to the previously mentioned two Vulcans, XJ783 arrived at Coningsby (7 November 1962) and was allocated to No. 9 Sqn. This brought the Wing's strength to ten Vulcans, with both squadrons operating five aircraft each. No. 9 Sqn's aircraft displayed either the large green 'bat' insignia on the tail fin, e.g. XL385, or the squadron badge on the side of the aircraft's nose beneath the observation window, e.g. XL386.

Across at Scampton, No. 27 Sqn began to exchange its earlier B.Mk2s for new Blue Steel aircraft, with XL444, XL445, XL446, XM569 and XM570 being taken on board, its five existing B.Mk2s vacated Scampton and were allocated to other Units. No. 230 OCU at Finningley received XH555 and XH556, whilst XJ823, XJ824 and XJ825 all made their way to Coningsby to join the new Wing.

No. 35 Squadron became the third Unit to form at Coningsby on 1 December 1962, taking delivery of XJ823, its first B.Mk2 on 2 January 1963. XJ823 had previously been No. 27 Sqn's first Vulcan (21 April 1961) and became No. 44 Sqn's first Vulcan B.Mk2 (1 November 1966), when the Waddington Wing was in the process of exchanging its B.Mk1As for the more powerful B.Mk2. XJ825 joined No. 35 Sqn (4 February 1963) and soon began to display the squadron's 'winged horse' badge on its tail fin. No. 9 Sqn took delivery of XJ824 (25 February 1963), increasing its total to six aircraft.

In November 1962 when No. 83 Sqn exchanged its earlier B.Mk2s to form No. 12 Sqn, XH554 of No. 83 Sqn was transferred to the OCU at Finningley increasing its numbers still further. On 1 March 1963 XH562 of the OCU joined No. 35 Sqn at Coningsby becoming the Unit's third aircraft. XH562 returned to the OCU ten days later (11 March 1963), but came back to Coningsby to rejoin No. 35 Sqn (30 April 1963). Two months later (29 June 1963) XH562, complete with squadron markings, appeared at the Yeovilton Open Day on static display. Earlier in the month (6 June) XH563 of No. 12 Sqn left Coningsby to return to the manufacturers for a retrofit.

By May 1963 all three squadrons were operational at Coningsby, with a combined strength of fourteen Vulcan B.Mk2s: XH560, XH562, XH563, XJ780–3, XJ823–5, XL385, XL386, XL388 and XL390 (XH, XJ and XL).

In 1963 RAF Coningsby was granted the freedom of Boston, Lincolnshire (the station's parent town). To mark the occasion a formation of three Vulcans, represented by an aircraft from each of the station's squadrons, gave a flypast over the town. Included in the formation were XJ825 of No. 35 Sqn and XJ783 representing No. 9 Sqn. It would have been one of the following five Vulcans, XH560, XJ780, XJ781, XJ782 or possibly XH563, that represented No. 12 Sqn. Also during 1963 the name 'Mayflower III' had been painted on the nose of XL388 beneath the No. 9 Sqn badge. This aircraft was flown to Boston, Massachusetts by Sqn Ldr Ron Dick with a message of greetings to the Mayor from the City Council of Boston in Lincolnshire. The purpose of the flight was to celebrate the anniversary of the sailing of the original *Mayflower*.

On 21 August 1963 the last of twenty-six Blue Steel-equipped Vulcan B.Mk2s arrived at RAF Scampton (XM595, Production No. 59). With the Scampton Wing fully equipped, the next batch of Vulcans delivered could now be allocated to the Coningsby Wing. The sixtieth B.Mk2 (XM596) was taken off the production line for fatigue testing. The remaining twenty-nine B.Mk2s ordered were destined to carry the American Skybolt Air-Launched Ballistic missile (ALBM). Skybolt had been destined to become the main weapon in Britain's Nuclear Deterrent Force, with RAF Coningsby earmarked as one of the stations to operate the missile.

The previously mentioned fourteen (XH, XJ and XL) Vulcans of the Coningsby Wing were only preliminary, pending the arrival of the new aircraft (Production Nos 61–89, XM597–612 and XM645–57) equipped to carry Skybolt. The new Vulcans would arrive with strengthened internal wings, along with attachment points for the pylons and fitted with Olympus 301 series engines (20,000 lb st thrust). In the end Skybolt was cancelled before the first of these Vulcans entered service. Only XM597–612 received the complete attachment points together with the ducting for the coolant/wiring during production, which was required for the missiles and pylons.

The remainder (XM645–57) were only partially completed when they entered service. It was for this reason that XM597, XM598, XM607 and XM612 were selected for the Black Buck raids on the Falkland Islands in 1982, as these were the only remaining Vulcans from that production batch still in service in April 1982. These four aircraft were supplemented by XL391, which also had the full Skybolt attachment points and the 301 engines, but lacked some other pieces of equipment that the four previously mentioned aircraft already had fitted to them. A sixth Vulcan (XM654) was also allocated as a reserve aircraft for the Black Buck raids, but remained at Waddington along with XL391 during the Falkland's War.

As previously mentioned XH563 of No. 12 Sqn had left the Coningsby Wing to head back to Avro to receive a retrofit (6 June 1963). Eleven days before the arrival of XM597 onto No. 12 Sqn (27 August 1963), XJ780 of the same squadron moved across to Yorkshire joining the OCU (16 August 1963). XJ780 had taken up the vacant slot at Finningley after XL384 left the Unit (7 August 1963) to receive a retrofit in order to equip it to carry Blue Steel. Its Olympus 201 engines would also be changed to 301 series. The second Skybolt aircraft (XM598) also joined No. 12 Sqn (4 September 1963), returning its total to five Vulcan B.Mk2s.

On 19 September 1963 XH562 of No. 35 Sqn followed the footsteps of XJ780 to Finningley and rejoined the OCU. XL385 of No. 9 Sqn left the Coningsby Wing (1 October 1963) to return to Woodford for the same modifications as XL384. No. 9 Sqn's total now dropped back to five B.Mk2s. Two additional Vulcans joined the Coningsby Wing in the October, with both aircraft going to No. 35 Sqn, XM599 (1 October 1963) and XM600 (3 October). The next exchange came at the beginning of November when XL386 left No. 9 Sqn, returning to Woodford for a retrofit on the 4th, with its replacement XM601 arriving for No. 9 Sqn the next day. Also in November, XM602 was allocated to No. 12 Sqn on the 11th and eighteen days later XH560 left the squadron to rejoin the OCU. On 2 December 1963, XJ824 left No. 9 Sqn and transferred to the OCU, replacing and allowing XL387 at Finningley to depart for Woodford on the same day to receive a retrofit. XJ824's slot at Coningsby with No. 9 Sqn was filled by XM603 two days later (4 December 1963). Arriving on the same day at Coningsby as XM603 was XM604, which had been allocated to No. 35 Sqn. On 20 December 1963, XJ782 followed the other ex-No. 12 Sqn Vulcans by going across to Finningley for the OCU. XJ782's replacement came ten days later, when XM606 joined No. 12 Sqn (30 December 1963). Also arriving on the same day as XM606 was XM605 for No. 9 Sqn. At the end of 1963 the Coningsby Wing had sixteen Vulcan B.Mk2s stationed

Figure 3.1:
XM597 became the first 301 series B.Mk2 to be delivered to the Coningsby Wing and the first to enter service equipped with the Skybolt attachment points. The aircraft is seen displaying the markings of No. 12 Sqn. (APN)

there, equipping the three squadrons. No. 9 Sqn had XJ783, XL388, XL390, XM601, XM603 and XM605. No. 12 Sqn's allocation was XJ781, XM597, XM598, XM602 and XM606. The five remaining aircraft allocated to No. 35 Sqn were XJ823, XJ825, XM599, XM600 and XM604.

On the first day of the new year XM607 arrived to join No. 35 Sqn. Having received XM605 on 30 December 1963, XL388 departed Coningsby for Woodford on 2 January 1964 for a retrofit and modifications to carry Blue Steel (XL384–90 all received similar modifications to carry Blue Steel). At the end of January both XM608 and XM609 arrived on the 29th for Nos 9 and 12 Sqns respectively. Six days after No. 12 Sqn received XM609, the last of the squadron's Olympus 201 series Vulcans XJ781, left the Unit to join...? You've guessed it, 'No. 230 OCU at Finningley' (4 February 1964). XJ781 was the replacement for XL389, which left the OCU to go back to Avro at Woodford on the same day. Over the next four weeks No. 9 Sqn took delivery of three further aircraft, XM610 (12 February 1964), XM611 (14 February 1964) and XM612 (3 March 1964). One of No. 9 Sqn's remaining Olympus 201 series Vulcans, XJ783, was involved in a flying accident on 23 February 1964. After receiving repairs, XJ783 was allocated to 'No 230 OCU at Finningley' (28 February 1964). XL390 was the last 201 series aircraft of No. 9 Sqn to leave the Coningsby Wing for Woodford on 2 March 1964, a day before XM612 arrived.

So far the seventy-six Vulcan B.Mk2s, including those involved in development work, had all been painted anti-flash white (with the exception of XM596, which was the fatigue test specimen). The final thirteen Vulcans would enter service with the two-tone upper surface camouflage (XM645–57). At this point the majority of the Vulcans in service lacked the flight-refuelling probe fitted to the aircraft's nose. Vulcans of the Coningsby Wing noted with the flight-refuelling probe fitted whilst in the original white colour scheme were: XM603, XM604, XM606, XM607 and

Figure 3.2:
*Four Vulcan B.Mk2s
of the Coningsby
Wing positioned on
the Operational
Readiness Platform
at RAF Wittering in
1964. The nearest
aircraft XM604
represents No. 35 Sqn
(note the fitting of
the Loran antenna
on the nose wheel
door and the flight-
refuelling probe). The
remaining three air-
craft are XM601 of
No. 9 Sqn, XM602
displaying the mark-
ings of No. 12 Sqn
and possibly XM603,
also from No. 9 Sqn.
Although it cannot be
seen, the latter air-
craft had a flight-
refuelling probe
fitted. (APN)*

XM612. The latter had been identified at one point displaying the Boston coat of arms (Tattershall Castle) on its tail fin.

The first camouflaged Vulcan XM645 arrived on 12 March 1964, nine days after the arrival of XM612. XM645 had been in service for only three months when it was involved in a Cat 3 flying accident (12 June 1964). None of the camouflaged Vulcans carried any squadron markings, but all of them (XM645–57) were fitted with flight-refuelling probes. Arriving on the 8 and 15 April were XM646 and XM647, delivered to Nos 12 and 35 Sqns respectively. On the last day of April, XJ825 of No. 35 Sqn followed the other XH and XJ 201 series Vulcans by going to Finningley for the OCU. By May 1964 only one of the preliminary 201 series Vulcans remained in service at Coningsby, it being XJ823 of No. 35 Sqn. It was on 11 May 1964 that XJ823 left the Coningsby Wing in the same fashion as the other earlier Vulcans by joining the OCU.

Figure 3.3:
*Taken on the same
occasion as Figure
3.2, this shot depicts
XM602 of No. 12
Sqn. Notice that the
Loran antenna has
yet to be fitted and
on close inspection it
is possible to see the
small 'coolant' blister
just ahead of the
twin Skybolt attach-
ment points. (APN)*

Figure 3.4:
Displaying the new two-tone upper surface camouflage scheme is XM600 (Wethersfield, 1964). This photo shows the extension of the green camouflage over the top of the exhaust pipes, although this was not always the case during the mid-1960s. (APN)

All of the XH and XJ aircraft had followed a similar route by first equipping the Scampton Wing with the B.Mk2 (1960/61). Second, they began to equip the Coningsby Wing with the B.Mk2 (1962/63) and then transferred to the OCU to increase numbers. This allowed the original Vulcan B.Mk2s issued to the OCU to be taken out of service to receive a manufacturer's retrofit (updated radars, jammers, sensors, etc.). The XH and XJ aircraft would then in turn receive a retrofit themselves before being used to equip the Waddington Wing, replacing the B.Mk1As.

Between May and October 1964 a further seven Vulcans joined the Coningsby Wing, XM648 (6 May 1964), XM649 (14 May), XM652 (12 August) and XM653 (4 September) all of which were issued to No. 9 Sqn. The remaining three joined No. 12 Sqn, XM650 (5 June 1964), XM651 (22 June) and XM654 (26 October).

On 19 September 1964 four Vulcans of the Coningsby Wing appeared at the Battle of Britain Open Day at RAF Finningley. The four aircraft were positioned on the station's operational readiness platforms poised ready to scramble, starting with XM601 and followed rapidly down the runway by XM604, XM605 and XM646. All four aircraft were fitted with flight-refuelling probes and displayed the low-level camouflage colour scheme that eventually was to become standard.

Only eighteen days after this event XM601, flown by a No. 9 Sqn crew, which included the squadron's Commanding Officer, Wg Cdr K. J. L. Baker, was written off when it crashed on approach to its home base at Coningsby on 7 October 1964. All five of the crew members were sadly

Figure 3.5:
*XM601 at RAF
Finningley on 19
eptember 1964
now fitted with the
flight-refuelling
probe. (APN)*

killed in the accident.

The following month would see dramatic changes. Orders had been given to move the entire Wing from Coningsby to RAF Cottesmore in Rutland. At the time of the move in November three of No. 12 Sqn's aircraft, XM597, XM606 and XM609, were out of service receiving manufacturer's modifications. Also at about this point the first Far East deployment of the Vulcan B.Mk2s took place under the operation name 'Chamfrom' during the Indonesian confrontation. The four Vulcans selected would take over from four Victor B.Mk1As of No. XV Sqn. No. 12 Sqn at Coningsby would carry out the deployment taking over the responsibility from the Victors on 30 September 1964. No. 12 Sqn's remaining aircraft before the deployment were: XM598, XM602, XM646, XM650, XM651 and XM654. The four Vulcans making the deployment (No. 12(B) Sqn) were all camouflaged and fitted with flight-refuelling probes, so presumably involved XM646, XM650, XM651 and XM654. This would have left XM598 and XM602 remaining at Coningsby along with sixteen other Vulcans of the Wing in service to make the move to Cottesmore in November.

On 23 November 1964 XM655 entered service initially with No. 9 Sqn at Cottesmore followed by the final two Vulcan B.Mk2s, XM656 (16 December 1964) and XM657 (15 January 1965); both aircraft were issued to No. 35 Sqn.

During the existence of the Coningsby Wing the three squadrons had been assigned free-fall duties using Yellow Sun Mk2 nuclear weapons.

04

Equipping the Waddington Wing with the B.Mk2

During 1965 the Waddington Wing was made up of Nos 44, 50 and 101 Sqns operating the Vulcan B.Mk1A. Their main offensive weapon was the yellow sun Mk2 nuclear weapon that required the aircraft to pop-up to at least 12,000 ft for release. At the beginning of 1966 No. 50 Sqn began to exchange its B.Mk1As for the B.Mk2 armed with the WE177B low-level parachute-retarded nuclear weapon.

THE FIRST VULCAN B.MK2 delivered to the Waddington Wing was XJ783 arriving on 3 January 1966. This was followed by a further sixteen B.Mk2s delivered over the next twenty months. Nine aircraft arrived during 1966 whilst the remaining eight arrived the following year.

On 8 February 1966 XH557 joined the Wing followed by XJ781 on 10 February, XJ782 (25 March), XL446 (16 September), XL445 (30 September), XJ824 (4 October), XJ823 (1 November) and XM569 (17 November). Inside No. 44 Sqn's operational record book, the first written entry showing the B.Mk2 alongside the B.Mk1As indicates XJ823 as being its first B.Mk2.

The first Vulcan to arrive at Waddington in 1967 was XM570 on 2 January, with XM572 following on 8 February (although indicated as returning to the Scampton Wing at that time), XH562 (10 February) XH560 (10 April), XJ825 (11 April), XM573 (25 April) and XM571 (3 July, ex-Cottesmore Wing). The seventeenth aircraft to join the Wing was XH561 arriving on 7 August 1967. There were now sufficient Vulcan B.Mk2s to equip both Nos 50 and 44 Sqns (XH557, XH560–2, XJ781–3, XJ823–5, XL445, XL446, XM569–73).

All of the above aircraft were fitted with 17,000 lb st. Olympus 201

Figure 4.1: *XM569, Captained by Flt Lt Allan Chapman of No. 50 Sqn, after its arrival at Royal Australian Air Force, Butterworth, Malaysia on 21 April 1967. The port foot brake motor had seized applying full pressure to port bogie. All tyres burst on touchdown and the brakes remained on maximum pressure. Notice the 'skid marks', abnormal tracks on the left and normal on the right. The aircraft was participating in a joint Waddington/Cottesmore Wing exercise 'Moonflower' (UK–Far East, Eastbound). Two of the Cottesmore Wing Vulcans known to have taken part in this deployment were XM600 and XM647.* **(RAAF Copyright Reserved)**

Figure 4.2:
XM569 depicted as an open top model. The canopy was jettisoned on landing in case the undercarriage collapsed, which would have prevented the crew from escaping. Close inspection at the tip of the aircraft's nose reveals that XM569 already had the radome modified to accept the Terrain-Following Radar, although not yet fitted on this occasion (notice the black cap/fairing over the tip of the nose).
(RAAF Copyright Reserved)

Figure 4.3:
'The offending bogie', but what is not visible are the wheels that were worn down to virtually a half circle.
(RAAF Copyright Reserved)

series engines, with the exception of XH557 that was fitted with Olympus 301 series engines rated at 20,000 lb st. This aircraft served its first four years (21 June 1960–1 July 1964) with the Ministry of Aviation on engine trials testing these more powerful engines. XH557 was then returned to Woodford for over a year where improvements were made to existing radars, jammers and sensors, as well as receiving additional equipment. The aircraft then entered service with the Cottesmore Wing for two months (6 December 1965–8 February 1966) to assist in providing the necessary cover for those Vulcans currently out of service receiving manufacturer's modifications, an example being XM645 (8 December 1965–17 February 1966). Five further Vulcans had been assigned the same task: XH560, XH562, XJ824, XJ825 and XM571. These aircraft served at Cottesmore for varying periods between August 1965 and July 1967 in order to help maintain individual squadron numbers of eight aircraft each. XM610, XM647, XM648 and XM655 are also examples of Cottesmore Wing aircraft that received manufacturer's modifications during that period. XH557 along with the four previously mentioned 201 series Vulcans were then transferred to the Waddington Wing.

Each of the XH and XJ aircraft issued to the Wing with the exception of XH557 had all previously served with No. 230 OCU at Finningley. The six XL and XM serial Vulcans had all been operating out of Scampton

Figure 4.4:
Vulcans of No. 50 Sqn at Luqa, Malta for 'Sunspot' ADEX (Air Defence Exercise) during October 1967. The flight line consists of XM569, XJ781, XL446, XM572, XM570, XH560 and XJ782. Notice the kangaroo, painted by the Australians at Butterworth in April 1967, on the tail fin of XM569 after the 'ploughing match' (seeFigures 4.2 and 4.3). (CBV)

with Blue Steel capability. These Vulcans then returned to the manufacturer for a retrofit, taking on average twelve months to complete before
being delivered to the Waddington Wing to replace the B1As one by one,
e.g. XJ824 arrived on 4 October 1966 then only eight days later XH501
departed for St Athan (12 October 1966). Similarly, XJ823 arrived on
1 November and nine days later XH480 left for St Athan (10 November
1966) and XM573 arrived on 25 April 1967 then seven days later XH476 set
off for St Athan (2 May). Upon arrival these B1As were declared as non-
effective airframes and stored before being sold for scrap approximately
two years later.

The final phase in equipping the Waddington Wing with the B.Mk2
occurred at the end of 1967. After a major rethink of Britain's nuclear
deterrent due to the cancellation of Skybolt, the planned transfer of
responsibility to the Royal Navy with Polaris missile-equipped submarines signalled the start of the slow rundown of the Vulcan Force. The

*Figure 4.5: A rather interesting picture due to it being taken at the time that the 201 series aircraft were being exchanged
with the 301 series between Waddington and Cottesmore. The four Vulcans are XH561 (nearest), XJ782, XM656 and XJ824.
The date was Tuesday, 26 March 1968 and the points to note are the station and Unit markings on the entrance door,
Terrain-Following Radar modification on all four aircraft (circular cap/fairing on tip of nose) but fitted to XH561 only,
301 series exhaust pipes on XM656 together with the updated yellow symbols and 'white square' on the emergency equipment panel.* **(Lincolnshire Echo)**

Craig Bulman

first casualty was No. 12 Sqn at Cottesmore that was earmarked to disband on 31 December 1967.

Cottesmore's two surviving squadrons (Nos 9 and 35) remained at their Rutland base, whilst across in Lincolnshire at Waddington Nos 44, 50 and 101 Sqns also remained stationed there, but the individual Vulcans did not. All of the Olympus 201 series aircraft headed for Cottesmore whilst the 301 series aircraft (XM597–612 and XM645–57) apart from XM646 and XM647 made the reverse journey to Waddington. Two of these Vulcans, XM601 and XM604, had both been written-off in accidents before the transfer took place. XM604 had been written off on 30 January 1968 when the aircraft crashed at Cow Close Farm whilst overshooting at Cottesmore with a fire in No. 2 engine. The Capt Flt Lt Peter Tait and his Co-Pilot, Fg Off M. Gillett, escaped after ejecting but the four remaining rear crew members were lost in the crash.

The first of the twenty-five Vulcans to make the journey to Waddington was XM645 on 14 December 1967 (arriving from St Athan), with XM600 being the last aircraft to transfer five months later on 30 May 1968. (For all of the individual dates of transfer for the remaining twenty-

Figure 4.6: *XH500 was one of the last eight Vulcan B.Mk1As to serve with the Waddington Wing in 1967, until being flown to Scampton in November of that year. This aircraft was then used for weapon-loading practice (1 January 1968– 29 September 1976) before being placed onto the station's fire dump pictured here in August 1977. Notice the day-glow elephant (rear view) painted on the tail fin (closely resembles that used by No. 27 Sqn during 1970).* **(Author's collection)**

three aircraft, see Chapter V).

With this extra capacity at Waddington, No. 101 Sqn began to convert to the more powerful B.Mk2 version. The Waddington Wing was now fully equipped with the B.Mk2. During the time that the B.Mk2s had been stationed at this Lincolnshire base each had the station badge, along with the three appropriate squadron badges, painted on the crew entrance door. The final three B.Mk1As to be taken out of service were XH502, XH505 and XH506. On 9 January 1968 XH505 was taken to Finningley where it was placed on the station's dump. This was followed by XH506 that left for St Athan on 10 January 1968 and on the same day XH502 had been allocated to the Waddington dump, with the nose section removed for crew training.

Throughout the latter part of 1967 and during 1968 four Vulcans equipped with Olympus 201 series engines were allocated to the Waddington Wing to assist in maintaining the appropriate squadron's strength, whilst others were out of service for manufacturer's modifications. The first of these was XJ780 (ex-No. 230 OCU) arriving on 10 October 1967 and remaining until 6 December 1968. The second aircraft XH563 operated with the Wing for eight months (6 August 1968–18 March 1969) before returning to the OCU. XM571, which had supplemented aircraft of the Cottesmore Wing in 1967 (20 January–3 July and 13 September–15 December), would now help to maintain the numbers at Waddington during 1968 (manufacturer's modifications 18 January–29 February 1968). The fourth aircraft XH558 (ex-No. 230 OCU) arrived on 26 February 1968 and remained with the Wing until 17 August 1973 (displayed the words 'starship enterprise' on the crew entrance door, c.1972). At that point the aircraft was flown to the manufacturer's facilities at Bitteswell for conversion by Hawker Siddley to B.Mk2 MRR standard before being issued to No. 27 Sqn at Scampton. XH558 had been the first Vulcan B.Mk2 to enter service with the RAF at Waddington when it joined No. 230 OCU on 1 July 1960. It ultimately became the very last Vulcan to fly, landing at Bruntingthorpe Leicestershire on 23 March 1993 to be preserved in serviceable condition for fast taxiing. In the meantime we can only hope and keep our fingers crossed that at some point in the future XH558 may be allowed to take to the skies and fly once again.

Plate 1: On 2 September 1978, whilst the previously mentioned OCU display crew, pictured on p.18, was in Germany displaying XL359, a further OCU crew was at RAF Leuchars where XH562 was on static display at the 'Battle of Britain at Home Day'. (**John Huggon**) (See text p.18)

Plate 2: Seen at RAF Leuchars in Scotland on 14 September 1968 is XL389 of the Scampton Wing. Notice the station badge together with the three Blue Steel squadrons painted on the crew entrance door. By looking above the rear of the missile it is possible to see the blisters indicating the location of the anti-icing unit for the 301 series engines. (John Huggon) (See text, p.31)

Plate 3: Having received No. 617 Sqn's new insignia, XL317 was put on static display at the Battle of Britain Day at Finningley on 18 September 1971. Notice that the insignia has been placed 'close' to the leading edge of the tail fin on this aircraft. (**John Huggon**) (See text, p.71)

Plate 4: XJ783 of No. 617 Sqn on detachment to RAF Leeming on 16 October 1979. Four further aircraft, XL392, XL426, XL446 and XM574, of No. 617 Sqn were also present at Leeming on the same day. (**Author's collection**) (See text, p.78)

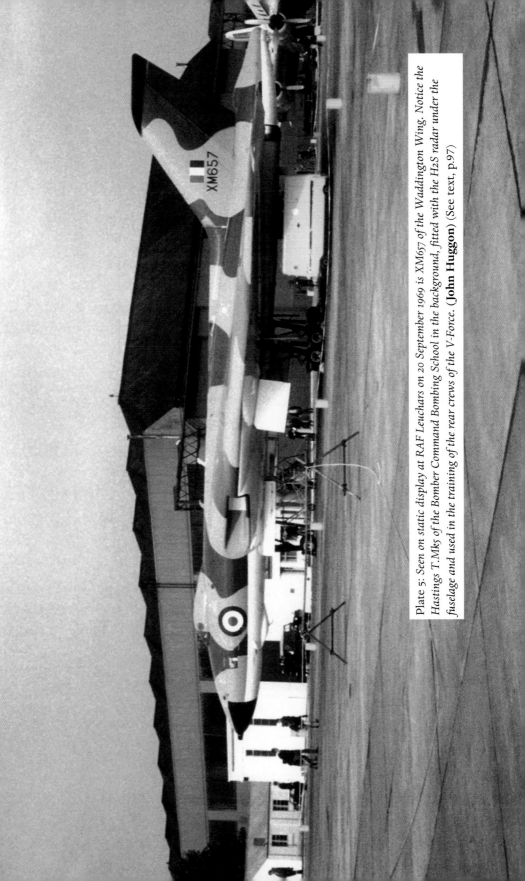

Plate 5: *Seen on static display at RAF Leuchars on 20 September 1969 is XM657 of the Waddington Wing. Notice the Hastings T.Mk5 of the Bomber Command Bombing School in the background, fitted with the H2S radar under the fuselage and used in the training of the rear crews of the V-Force.* (**John Huggon**) (*See text, p.97*)

Plate 6: Vulcan B.Mk2 XM609 of the Waddington Wing, seen during a display at Prestwick on 3 June 1972. Notice that the aircraft has received the modified version of the 'X band jammer' together with the new VHF aerials but has not yet been repainted and therefore lacks the 'white square' background for the first-aid cross, on the emergency equipment bay panel (see Chapter 10). (**John Huggon**) (See text, p.101)

Plate 7: *After taking part in a scramble take-off along with XL387, XM612 is seen here climbing away from Finningley on 8 September 1973. Notice that the aircraft has now been fitted, under the bulged tail section, with the modified 'X band jammer' (two emitter heads).* (See text, p.102) (**John Huggon**)

Plate 8: *Seen on the ORP at Finningley on 30 July 1977 is XL389 displaying No. 9 Sqn's 'bat' insignia together with the Lincoln coat of arms. Notice the 'fuzzy edge' to the green paint on the rudder (probably a replacement).* (**John Huggon**) (See text, p.109)

Plate 9: Seen at Leuchars on 10 September 1977 is XM606 (sicky-o-sicky) of No. 101 Sqn. Notice the pale background colour inside the squadron's insignia depicting a lion in a turret. This badge was later revised to show the lions head along and one paw in the turret with its tail extending outside of the numeral '101'. (**John Huggon**) (See text, p.113)

Plate 10: Four Vulcan B.Mk2s, XH559 No. 35 Sqn, XM651 No. 50 Sqn, XM609 No. 44 Sqn, XM646 No. 9 Sqn, on static display at RAF Finningley on 29–30 July 1977 for the Queen's Silver Jubilee celebrations. All four aircraft have received passive ECM tail fairing (radar warning receiver) giving the tail section a square look. Notice that the camouflage extends over the top section of the tail fin (previously black), although there are a number of aircraft which received the passive ECM tail whilst retaining the black, e.g. XH562 No. 44 Sqn 1976. (QAPI) (See text p.169)

The Cottesmore Wing

I N NOVEMBER 1964 the Cottesmore Wing came into existence by relocating Nos 9, 12 and 35 Sqns from RAF Coningsby in Lincolnshire to its new Rutland base. All three of the squadrons were operating the Vulcan B.Mk2 and had been assigned free-fall duties using Yellow Sun Mk2 nuclear weapons. On 15 January 1965 the final Vulcan B.Mk2 (XM657) entered service with the Cottesmore Wing and joined No. 35 Sqn. At this point only twenty-eight of the final twenty-nine production Vulcan B.Mk2s, fitted with Olympus 301 engines, were attached to the Cottesmore Wing (XM597–600, XM602–12 and XM645–57). The missing aircraft out of the sequence was XM601, which had been written off after crashing whilst on approach to RAF Coningsby's main runway on 7 October 1964, with the loss of all the crew.

In December 1964 the four Vulcan B.Mk2s of No. 12 (B) Sqn returned to Cottesmore, having completed a two-month detachment to the Far East ('Operation Chamfrom'). Soon all the aircraft would have the Cottesmore station badge painted on the crew entrance door, along with the three appropriate squadron markings (Nos 9, 12 and 35 Sqns). The new Wing would also become the first to operate with the new WE177B lay-down strategic nuclear weapon. This change came about after the cancellation of its intended weapon — Skybolt.

It was the squadrons at Cottesmore that were assigned with future deployments to the Far East during the Indonesian confrontations. In April 1965 No. 35 Sqn had been tasked with a practice reinforcement of the Far East. 'Exercise Spherical', as it would be known, required the deployment of eight Vulcan B.Mk2s to the Far East. After only forty-two hours from the request for reinforcements, the Vulcans had reached their initial staging post at Gan in the Indian Ocean. The eight aircraft, which included XM597, XM598, XM599, XM600, XM603, XM604 and XM605, were then positioned forward, with four of the Vulcans going to Tengah and the remaining four to Butterworth. Three of the four aircraft that flew on to Butterworth were XM600, XM603 and XM605. Exercise

Spherical showed that the Vulcans being deployed from the UK could be on their targets in the Far East only forty-eight hours after the request for reinforcements.

At least four aircraft (Vulcan/Victor) were retained in the Far East during the confrontations to ensure that all pre-planned principal targets were covered. In August 1965 No. 57 Sqn operating four Victor B.Mk1As stationed at Tengah, Singapore returned to the UK. Their position in the Far East was taken over by No. 9 Sqn on the 13th August. In early March 1966 No. 35 Sqn returned to the Far East to take over the commitment from No. 9 Sqn. The aircraft and aircrew were rotated every four months. This was known as the 'Matterhorn Rotation'.

Throughout the deployment to the Far East by Cottersmore's Vulcans occasional air defence exercises (ADEX) would take place. The exercises involved the Royal Australian Air Force using its Canberra, Mirage and Sabre aircraft. Over two years, four ADEX took place. The first exercise (High Rigel) occurred in December 1965 followed by the second (Short Spica) in March 1966. Five months passed before the third exercise known as 'High Castor' took place. The fourth exercise (High Mars) did not take place until November 1967. Targets normally included Darwin in Northern Australia as well as Tindal Air Base situated about 200 miles to the south of Darwin. It was during High Castor on 14 August 1966 that the Bangkok agreement was signed, bringing an end to the confrontation between Malaysia and Indonesia. By keeping a presence in the Far East and being prepared to act, the V-Force had played its part in bringing this episode to its conclusion. The final two Vulcans to be withdrawn from the Far East at the end of the confrontation were XM610 and XM612 (30 August 1966).

Figure 5.1: *Members of No. 35 Sqn whilst on detachment to Tengah, Singapore, under the command of Sqn Ldr Eric Stacey. This photo was taken at the end of the long confrontation between Malaysia and Indonesia in August 1966. XM657 was one of the first two Vulcans to be withdrawn from the Far East, the other being XM645 (both aircraft arrived back at Cottesmore on 26 August 1966). XM657 was also one of the three Vulcans that had taken part in 'High Castor' (air defence exercise) during August.* **(CBV via Rusty Russell)**

Craig Bulman

As mentioned previously, the Cottesmore Wing was equipped with twenty-eight Vulcans, all of which had Olympus 301 series engines (January 1965). With three squadrons operating eight aircraft each, this left them with four spare. At any one time there would be up to seven Vulcans out of service receiving manufacturer's modifications, including XM606 that had been loaned to the Ministry of Aviation (14 June 1965–2 May 1967). To fill the gap and help maintain squadron strength, several Vulcans with 201 series engines saw service with the Wing. The first example of this was in August 1965 when XM600, XM603, XM604, XM606, XM651 and XM654 were all out of service receiving modifications (XM606, Ministry of Aviation). So, to fill the gap, XH562 was transferred from the OCU at Finningley (1 August 1965) and XH560, having just received a retrofit after previously serving with the OCU, joined the Cottesmore Wing (23 August 1965); thereby helping to maintain Wing's numbers at twenty-four. Across at Finningley the numbers on the OCU were maintained by the introduction into service of the two Skybolt test

Figure 5.2:
Note the four badges on the crew entrance door of XM599 of the Cottesmore Wing in 1965 depicting the station's badge and Nos 9, 12 and 35 Sqns. Also worth noting is the coolant blister together with the twin forward and single rear attachment points for the originally intended Skybolt missile pylon. **(APN)**

Figure 5.3:
XM611 is pictured at its home base in 1965 with a flight-refuelling probe fitted and the upper surface camouflage extending over the top of the exhaust pipes. **(APN)**

aircraft, XH537 and XH538, which had been allocated to the OCU at the end of May 1965. By mid-September there were seven aircraft out of service: XM600, XM603–6, XM612 and XM654. Arriving on 3 September 1965 (to fill the gap) was XJ825, an ex-OCU aircraft having just received a manufacturer's retrofit.

In November 1965 XH536 having spent its previous five-and-a-half years on trials, which included the Olympus 200 series engines, entered service with the Cottesmore Wing (24 November 1965). Eleven weeks later a No. 9 Sqn crew flying XH536 over Wales was unfortunate in that the aircraft struck the ground whilst conducting trials with the Terrain-Following Radar. None of the crew survived the crash, which happened at Fan-Bwlchchwtyth, Hedl-Senni in Wales (2 February 1966).

On 6 December 1965 XH557 with its Olympus 301 series engines, finally entered service with the RAF having also spent the first five-and-a-half years on engine trails with the Ministry of Aviation. XH557 joined the Cottesmore Wing and remained with it for three months before being allocated to the Waddington Wing. This Vulcan became the second B.Mk2 issued to the Waddington Wing, continuing the process of replacing the earlier B.Mk1As.

One of the earlier 201 series Vulcans 'XH560' was out of service itself for four weeks (4 February–2 March 1966) for manufacturer's modifications. Six days after XH560 returned to the Wing, XH562 left for modifications but did not return until 15 December. Whilst XH562 was away XJ824 joined the Wing for a three-month stay (4 July–4 October 1966). During July 1966 seven aircraft were out of service: XM611 XM646, XM647, XM649, XM650, XM656 (manufacturer's modifications) and XM597, whose undercarriage had collapsed (Cat 3 FA, 23 June 1966). With three 201 series Vulcans in service with the Wing at that time, XH560, XJ824 and XJ825, the number of aircraft on strength remained at twenty-four.

At the start of 1967 there were three 201 series Vulcans operating at Cottesmore: XH560, XH562 and XJ825, but on 12 January 1967 XH560 began to receive further modification work and returned to service on 22 March 1967. By that time both XH562 and XJ825 had left Cottesmore to join the Waddington Wing and in so doing helped to replace more of the B.Mk1As. XH562 transferred on 10 February 1967, whilst XJ825 initially received manufacturer's modifications starting on 3 February 1967 before being transferred to Waddington just over two months later on 11 April. After receiving a retrofit and conversion from Blue Steel back to free-fall bombing, XM571 was assigned to the Cottesmore Wing (20 January 1967). When XH560 finally left the Wing to also go across to

Figure 5.4:
XM656 is shown demonstrating the release of twenty-one 1,000 lb live retarded bombs in front of an invited audience on Salisbury Plain in 1967. **(APN)**

Waddington (10 April 1967) only one 201 series Vulcan remained at Cottesmore (XM571). With only XM602, XM606, XM612, XM645 and XM653 out of service in April 1967, XM571 would have been sufficient to maintain the Wing's strength at twenty-four. XM571 moved over to Waddington on 3 July 1967 for two months to cover for XJ824, which left Waddington on the same day to receive modification work. XM571 returned to the Cottesmore Wing on 13 September 1967.

By the end of the year there would be big changes in the V-Force due to the cancellation of Skybolt and the planned transfer of nuclear responsibility to the Royal Navy. There would then be a surplus of aircraft and squadrons in the V-Force. The first Vulcan squadron to become a casualty of this policy was No. 12 Sqn at Cottesmore, which had been earmarked to disband at the end of the year (31 December 1967).

With the disbandment of No. 12 Sqn there would be a surplus number of Vulcan B.Mk2s at Cottesmore. Whilst across at Waddington there were three squadrons (Nos 44, 50 and 101), but only two were equipped with the B.Mk2. The appropriate decision had been taken to move all of the 301 engine Vulcans at Cottesmore (XM597–612 and XM645–57) across to Waddington, with the exception of XM646 and XM647, then transfer all of the 201 engine Vulcans from Waddington to Cottesmore. Prior to the disbandment of No. 12 Sqn, four Vulcans made the move to Waddington. XM645 transferred on 14 December, followed by XM571 (201 series) on the 15th, XM650 and XM652 on the 19th and 24th respectively. In January 1968 a further six Vulcans moved across to Waddington, the aircraft involved were: XM599 (on the 9th), XM655 (12th), XM603 and XM649 (both 18th), XM653 (24th), and XM648 (25th). Only two Vulcans

Figure 5.5:
*Having previously
served at Scampton,
Conningsby,
Finningley and
Waddington, XJ824
is positioned on the
operational readiness
platform at the Battle
of Britain display at
Finningley on
14 September 1968,
then serving with the
Cottesmore Wing.
(APN)*

made the reverse journey, XM569 (19 January 1968) and XM570 (25 January 1968). At this point the Waddington Wing had gained eight additional aircraft, having received ten and handing over only two of its 201 series Vulcans to Cottesmore. The Waddington Wing now had the extra capacity to equip No. 101 Sqn with the B.Mk2.

On 30 January 1968 XM604 of the Cottesmore Wing was written off after the No. 2 engine had caught fire, resulting in the aircraft crashing at Cow Close Farm whilst practising an ILS approach and overshoot at Cottesmore. The Pilot and Co-Pilot escaped but the four remaining rear crew members were lost in the crash.

The remaining sixteen 301 series Vulcans transferred across to Waddington over the following four months. On 2 February 1968 XH560 returned to serve once again at Cottesmore, with XM656 making the reverse journey to Waddington on the same day. Throughout February and March 1968 six more aircraft transferred at a rate of three per month. The aircraft making the move in February were XM610, XM605 and XM608 (5th, 16th and 27th respectively). The three Vulcans that made the move in March were XM612 (on the 5th), XM609 (8th) and XM657 (19th). Only one aircraft per month made the reverse journey during the same period to join the Cottesmore Wing, XJ825 arrived on 19 February 1968 and XJ783 (the first B.Mk2 allocated to the Waddington Wing) transferred on 22 March 1968. During April eleven aircraft were exchanged: XM572, XJ782, XL445, XJ781, XH562 and XJ823 (5th, 9th, 18th, 22nd, 24th and 29th respectively). The 301 series Vulcans making their way across to Waddington were: XM598, XM597, XM602, XM651 and XM654 (9th, 18th 24th, 24th and 30th respectively). In May the final four aircraft transferred to Waddington starting with XM606 on the 13th, followed by XM607 (24th), XM611 (28th) and XM600 (30th). On 8 May 1968 XH561 became the twelfth 201 series Vulcan to transfer from Waddington to Cottesmore.

The penultimate Vulcan to complete the initial exchange of aircraft between the two stations was XJ824 on 19 June 1968 pending the transfer of XJ780 six months later.

Two further aircraft, XH558 and XH563, transferred from the OCU at Finningley to join the Waddington Wing on 26 February 1968 and 6 August 1968 respectively. XH563 had been sent to Waddington in exchange for XM645 (301 series) that flew to Finningley to join the OCU on 5 August 1968. By August the Waddington Wing was equipped with twenty-nine Vulcans while Cottesmore had sixteen. As mentioned previously, two 301 series aircraft, XM646 and XM647, remained at Cottesmore. Thirteen 201 series aircraft had transferred from Waddington with XL391 (301 series) joining them on 31 July 1968 after spending its first five years on development work and a further year receiving modifications. The sixteen Vulcans now making up the Wing were: XH560–2, XJ781–3, XJ823–5, XL391, XL445, XM569, XM570, XM572, XM646 and XM647. On 6 December 1968 Cottesmore finally received an additional aircraft in the form of XJ780 from Waddington as mentioned above.

With all of the appropriate aircraft having been exchanged by the end of 1968 the Cottesmore Wing was about to enter its final phase. Nos 9 and 35 Sqns were soon to be moved from Cottesmore to Akrotiri in Cyprus where they would become known as the Near East Air Force Bomber Wing, replacing the four squadrons of Canberra's currently stationed there. Akrotiri would then become their third base in seven years.

The move to Cyprus would start in January 1969 and was due to be completed by March. Sixteen Vulcans would deploy in groups of four starting with No. 35 Sqn on 15 January whilst its remaining four aircraft would follow on 5 February. No. 9 Sqn's first four aircraft would depart Cottesmore on 26 February, followed by a further four, which included XM571 (ex-Waddington Wing) on 19 March 1969. This would leave two Vulcans remaining at Cottesmore waiting to be relocated (XJ780 and XJ781). The Cottesmore Wing came to an end when both aircraft were given new postings on 18 April 1969. XJ780 returned to the Waddington Wing to cover for XM612, which came out of service on the same day to receive manufacturer's modifications. Meanwhile XJ781 followed the same route as the others by going to the warmer and sunnier climate of Cyprus. During 1968 whilst serving with the Cottesmore Wing, XJ781 had been noted to have a Union Jack painted on its tail fin.

Throughout the existence of the Cottesmore Wing none of the aircraft carried any individual squadron markings on their tail fin due to the policy of centralized servicing. Although at one point several Vulcans were photographed at Tengah in Singapore displaying No. 9 Sqn's insignia, which was a green bat painted onto a yellow circular background with the Unit's number (IX) placed in the middle. Two of the Vulcans identified in this detachment were XM600 and XM610. Although the date of this detachment is unknown (possibly January 1968), the only period that these two aircraft were attached to No. 9 Sqn was whilst they were part of the Cottesmore Wing. Both of them transferred to the Waddington Wing during 1968 (XM600, 30 May and XM610, 5 February) when they were attached to Nos 44, 50 and 101 Sqns.

06

Near East Air Force Bomber Wing

From 1957 the RAF had stationed four squadrons of Canberras (Nos 6, 32, 73 and 249 Sqns) at Akrotiri in Cyprus. These aircraft formed the backbone of the Near East Air Force (NEAF) Strike Wing. In May 1968 a decision had been taken to replace the four Canberra squadrons with two squadrons of Vulcan B.Mk2s. Their aim would be to provide support for CENTO (Central Treaty Organisation) as well as continuing to support the UK's national interest. The deployment of the Vulcans would begin in January 1969. The squadrons selected were Nos 9 and 35, both of which were stationed at RAF Cottesmore. This would provide the force with greater flexibility due to the increased weapon load and range of the Vulcans.

OVER TWO MONTHS, beginning on 15 January 1969, the sixteen Vulcans would deploy to Akrotiri in groups of four. This deployment began with No. 35 Sqn sending XH560, XH562, XJ783 and XL445 from Cottesmore for the sunnier climate of Cyprus on the 15th. The squadron's remaining four aircraft, XJ823, XJ824, XL391 and XM646, followed on 5 February. Three weeks later on 26 February No. 9 Sqn deployed the first four of its aircraft to Cyprus: XJ825, XM569, XM570 and XM647. The final four aircraft, XH561, XJ782, XM571 and XM572, followed three weeks later on 19 March 1969. Prior to the deployment XM571 had served the previous twelve months with the Waddington Wing. The NEAF Bomber Wing was now equipped with sixteen Vulcan B.Mk2s, but still had no reserve aircraft. Back in the UK XJ780 and XJ781, which were both part of the Cottesmore Wing, would soon be given new postings. On 18 April 1969 XJ781 made the journey to Akrotiri whilst XJ780 rejoined the Waddington Wing where it had previously served from 10 October 1967 to 6 December 1968. Out of the seventeen Vulcans attached to the NEAF only three were fitted with Olympus 301 series engines (XL391, XM646 and XM647) whilst XL445, XM569, XM570, XM571 and XM572 were previously Blue Steel-equipped. For the remainder of 1969 the Wing's strength remained at seventeen. On 12 January 1970 an additional Vulcan was allocated to the Wing. This would allow the squadrons to maintain their strength whilst some of the original sixteen Vulcans returned to the UK for servicing and manufacturer's modifications (delivered to St Athan or Bitteswell via Waddington). The additional Vulcan was XJ780, flown out to Cyprus after serving with the Waddington Wing during 1969.

Two months later XJ823 became the first aircraft to return to the UK for manufacturer's modifications that took five months to complete (13 March–14 August 1970), with XJ824 following a month later (15 April–8 September 1970). Before the departure of the next Vulcan scheduled for manufacturer's modifications, two additional aircraft would join the Wing from No. 230 OCU at Scampton. XM573 arrived on 26 June 1970 followed by a 301 series Vulcan, XJ784, on 21 July 1970. The OCU had received two replacements for these aircraft in the form of XL319 and XL386. Both aircraft came from the Scampton Wing after being reconverted from Blue Steel back to conventional bombing. On 16 July 1970 XJ780 returned to the UK for manufacturer's modifications. This was only five days before the arrival at Akrotiri of XJ784, which remained in Cyprus until 16 December 1970 when it left to join the Waddington Wing. Two days later on the 18th, XJ780 completed its modifications/service and rejoined the NEAF.

During the second half of 1970 four more Vulcans left Cyprus to

Figure 6.1:
Showing their loyalty to No. IX Sqn are Flt Lt Colin Dodds and crew whilst on detachment to RAF Masirah, Sultanate of Oman on 18 December 1970 (notice the hand hiding No. 35 Sqn's badge). Behind them is XM572 of the Near East Air Force Bomber Wing (having just returned to service after the completion of its manufacturer's modifications). Notice the absence of the anti-icing unit exhaust 'blisters' indicating that this is a 201 series aircraft and the small coolant 'blister' under the wing. There were only three other aircraft with this permutation/features: XM570, XM571 and XM573 (NEAF December 1970).
(via Colin N. Dodds and John Huggon)

Craig Bulman

Figure 6.2:
Commanding Officer, Wg Cdr Ron Dick and the crews of No. IX Sqn grouped for the annual photograph in March 1971. The serial number can be partially seen on the nose wheel door with the final number hidden, but it is understood to be either XJ823 or XJ824.
(CBV via Colin N. Dodds and John Huggon)

Figure 6.3:
Taxiing into dispersal at its home base, Akrotiri, in March 1971 is Vulcan B.Mk2 XJ780. Five-and-a-half years later the aircraft was modified to B.Mk2 MRR standard to serve with No. 27 Sqn at Scampton.
(CBV via Colin N. Dodds and John Huggon)

Figure 6.4:
Photographed at Akrotiri are members of No. 9 Bomber Sqn (No. IX B Sqn). The ex-Blue Steel Vulcan in the background can be identified as either XL445 or XM569 (twin ECM plates, 201 series engines, clean wing 'no blisters', NEAF 1971). With further similar reference photos of either aircraft at about that time it would be possible to confirm which of the two it is by matching the camouflage.
(CBV via Rod Powell)

receive manufacturer's modifications: XH562 (7 August 1970–12 January 1971), XH561 (18 September 1970–28 January 1971), XJ825 (15 October 1970–9 March 1971) and XJ781 (5 December 1970–7 April 1971). After XJ781 arrived back at Akrotiri there would have been nineteen Vulcans allocated to the Wing. This total remained unaltered for three months. On 7 July 1971 XM572 returned to the UK for manufacturer's modifications, whilst XJ783 made the same journey on 6 December 1971. XM572 made the reverse journey to rejoin the NEAF eight days later, returning on 14 December (manufacturer's modifications completed on XJ783 on 28 March 1972). Making a second appearance on 18 August 1971 was XJ784. Apart from an absence in 1973 for manufacturer's modifications, XJ784 remained with the NEAF until the Wing's demise in 1975. There was one other movement in 1971 when XH560 left Cyprus on a one-way leg to the UK to be placed in storage (20 October 1971–1 February 1973). The aircraft then received a major service and conversion into a B.Mk2 MRR by Hawker Siddley at Bitteswell and was then delivered to No. 27 Sqn at Scampton on 15 March 1974. In 1982 the same aircraft was selected for conversion into a K2 tanker, operating with No. 50 Sqn at Waddington. XH560 certainly got around during its lifetime, serving at all the main Vulcan stations, e.g. No. 12 Sqn Coningsby 1963, No. 230 OCU Finningley 1964, Nos 9, 12 and 35 Sqns Cottesmore Wing 1965–66, Nos 44, 50 and 101 Sqns Waddington Wing 1967, Nos 9 and 35 Sqns Akrotiri 1969–71, and No. 27 Sqn Scampton 1974–82. At the end of 1971 the following eighteen aircraft were attached to the NEAF: XH561, XH562, XJ780–2, XJ784, XJ823–5, XL391, XL445, XM569, XM570–3, XM646 and XM647.

During 1972 two more Vulcans joined the NEAF having already received their manufacturer's modifications and remained with the Wing for the remainder of its existence. The first being XL443 (ex-No. 27 Sqn) on 12 April followed by XL446 (ex-SW) on 31 July.

Whilst on a visit to New Zealand in 1972 (RNZAF Station Ohakea) a No. 9 Sqn crew flying XH562 arrived at their aircraft one morning to find it had been 'zapped'. The roundel on the nose was now painted in RNZAF markings (red KIWI in the centre). The No. 9 Sqn crew was in New Zealand to collect a trophy representing the squadron's crest in the form of a bat, which had originally been presented to a previous serving officer of the squadron. After locating No. 9 Sqn in Cyprus, the officer's widow had offered the trophy back to them. During the visit XH562 gave numerous flying displays including the 1972 Hamilton Air Show. Throughout the trip the aircraft displayed the squadron's markings on its tail fin (a large green and yellow bat). Similar markings were applied to another of its Vulcans, XJ823, whilst participating in the 1972 bombing

Figure 6.5:
Representing the NEAF in the 1972 Strike Command Bombing Competition held at RAF Scampton during April was Flt Lt Colin Dodds and the crew of No. 9 Sqn. The primary NEAF aircraft selected to take part in the competition was XJ823, seen here at Scampton with the squadron's 'bat' insignia on the tail fin (XM572 was the reserve). Notice on the inset picture the 'fuzzy' edge to the green paint on the rudder, indicating a possible replacement.
(Colin N. Dodds via John Huggon)

and navigation competition.

By the end of July 1972 the number of Vulcans allocated to the NEAF had risen to twenty-one after the arrival of XL446 (31 July). The aircraft concerned were: XH561, XH562, XJ780–4, XJ823–5, XL391, XL443, XL445, XL446, XM569–73, XM646 and XM647 (XH562 is believed to have been at St Athan for a major service, delivered from St Athan to Waddington on 2 August 1972). One of the previously mentioned aircraft, XJ780, had been involved in a Cat 3 FA (19 July 1972) and was temporarily grounded for repairs. This large allocation of aircraft was short lived because over the coming weeks and months, four of the Vulcans were to return to the UK for manufacturer's modifications (about six months). The four aircraft were: XM571 (10 August 1972–13 January 1973), XM647 (31 August 1972–23 January 1973), XM570 (8 September 1972–7 March 1973) and XJ782 (11 November 1972–17 May 1973).

During 1973 more of the Vulcans received the new low-visibility red/blue roundels. Some of the aircraft were seen with light grey undersides and the 'white bib' (underside of the radome remained white).

Fate struck XJ781 on 23 May 1973 as it approached Shiraz in Iran when its port main undercarriage failed to lower. All of the No. 9 Sqn crew survived the landing on a foam strip, but the aircraft slid off the runway tearing off the nose wheel and starboard undercarriage legs. XJ781 was struck off charge on 27 May 1973 after being declared beyond repair.

Five further Vulcans left Akrotiri to receive manufacturer's modifications during 1973. At the end of January of that year XJ784 (301 engines) departed for the UK and returned seven months later (31 January–23 August 1973). This was only a week after XM647 (301 engines) returned to Cyprus (23 January). One week after XJ784 returned in August, XM646 (301 engines) departed (31 August 1973–22 March 1974), whilst XM569 had already left the NEAF Bomber Wing on 3 April 1973 on a one-way flight. Upon completion of the modifications in the UK XM569 was issued to the newly reformed No. 27 Sqn as a standard B.Mk2 (4 July 1974). On 1 May 1973 XM573 followed a similar pattern as XM569. After receiving modifications XM573 returned for a short tour of duty in Cyprus, before being issued to No. 27 Sqn, also as a standard B.Mk2 (manufacturer's modifications 1 May–23 November 1973, No. 27 Sqn 17 April 1974). The fifth Vulcan, XL391, left the Bomber Wing (28 December 1973) to return to the UK. An additional Vulcan arrived to join the Bomber Wing on 24 August 1973 in the form of XM574. This 301 engine Vulcan had served the past twenty-two months (including its time out for manufacturer's modifications) with the Waddington Wing.

On 8 May 1974 XM570 departed Akrotiri to start a new phase in its service life, transferring to No. 27 Sqn at Scampton as a standard B.Mk2. The aircraft would soon be displaying the squadron's insignia, depicting a side view of an Indian elephant on a white circular background. Four days after XM570 arrived at Scampton, XM645 (301 engines) departed Waddington for Akrotiri to take up the post with the NEAF (12 March 1974). Just over a month later on 17 April 1974, two Vulcans headed back to the UK. The first being the previously mentioned XM573 that transferred to No. 27 Sqn and the second being XH561 which returned for manufacturer's modifications. Two days later on 19 April 1974 a replacement (XH557, 301 engines) left the Waddington Wing to join the NEAF. At this point the Bomber Wing had six Vulcans with Olympus 301 engines: XH557, XJ784, XM574 and XM645–7. Only one more Vulcan (XH562) returned to the UK for manufacturer's modifications during 1974. When this aircraft departed on 16 July, the number of Vulcan B.Mk2s allocated to the Wing was seventeen. Only four days after XH562 had left Akrotiri in the south of Cyprus, the Turkish Forces invaded the north of the island. A political decision was taken to withdraw the two squadrons of Vulcans back to the UK (January 1975). Their permanent post in Cyprus was to be replaced by detachments from the UK-based squadrons. The first of these temporary postings began with four Vulcans of No. 50 Sqn from Waddington, arriving at Akrotiri on 20 January 1975.

When the Vulcans relocated in the UK No. 9 Sqn took up its post at RAF Waddington and No. 35 Sqn at RAF Scampton. With seventeen Vulcans in Cyprus and XL391 currently receiving manufacturer's modifications, they would have had a theoretical total of eighteen. Each squadron required eight aircraft and reserves were easier to locate as the entire Vulcan Force would be stationed at these two Lincolnshire bases. This meant that two aircraft were surplus to requirement. The process of relocating the eighteen Vulcans began with XM571 joining No. 27 Sqn at Scampton on 3 January 1975 in a similar fashion to three previously mentioned ex-NEAF Vulcans (XM569, XM570 and XM573). On 8 January 1975 XJ782 rejoined the Waddington Wing in which it had previously served during 1966 and 1967 when the B.Mk1As were being phased out in place of the B.Mk2s.

In a similar way to the original deployment in 1969 the sixteen remaining Vulcans would return in groups of four but over ten days. No. 9 Sqn began the process on 15 January by returning four of the 301 series Vulcans (XH557, XJ784, XM645 and XM647) back to Waddington. The following day, on the 16th, the first four of No. 35 Sqn's aircraft, all with 201 series engines, made their way to Scampton (XJ783, XJ825, XL445 and XL446). On 17 January the remaining four aircraft of No. 9 Sqn (XJ780, XJ823, XL391 and XM646) made the journey to Waddington, the latter two with 301 series engines. The remaining aircraft of No. 35 Sqn vacated Akrotiri a week later on 24 January 1975. This departure marked the end of the NEAF Bomber Wing and the end of an era. The final four Vulcans were XJ824, XL443, XM572 and XM574 (the latter with 301 series engines). Now that each squadron had its own aircraft and centralized servicing had ended, individual squadron markings could be reapplied to the Vulcans. In addition to these markings, aircraft stationed at Waddington also displayed the Lincolnshire coat of arms on the tail fin.

07

Continuing in Service in a New Era — Scampton

B Y THE END OF AUGUST 1969 there were eighty Vulcan B.Mk2s remaining from the original total of eighty-eight that flew. Two of these aircraft, XH533 and XH539, were still involved in trials with the A&AEE. The following eight Vulcans had already been written off in various air and ground accidents: XH535, XH536, XH555, XH556, XL385, XM576, XM601 and XM604. This now left a total of seventy-eight Vulcan B.Mk2s to continue in service with the RAF well into the next decade, as there was still plenty of life left in these magnificent aircraft.

Now that the Royal Navy held the mantel of responsibility for the nuclear deterrent it was decided to maintain the Vulcan B.Mk2 in service, with the seventy-eight aircraft being distributed between the OCU and the seven remaining squadrons. Naturally there would be a number of these Vulcans out of service for manufacturer's modifications along with those receiving servicing and repairs, after the squadrons had been allocated a total of eight aircraft each. The remaining Units were now all

Figure 7.1:
Avro Lancaster VII NX611 stands on guard at RAF Scampton's main gate (1977).
(Author's collection)

located at three key RAF stations, with Nos 27 and 617 Sqns along with No. 230 OCU at Scampton, Nos 44, 50 and 101 Sqns operating out of Waddington, and Nos 9 and 35 Sqns forming the NEAF Bomber Wing at Akrotiri in Cyprus.

Beginning with Scampton, once No. 83 Sqn had disbanded (29 August 1969) its aircraft could be returned to the manufacturer's facilities at Bitteswell to have their Blue Steel fittings removed and then replaced by the original bomb doors. No. 27 Sqn was now earmarked to retrain and convert to free-fall tactical nuclear and conventional bombing roles, in order to become operational in the new year. The squadron's first Vulcan might well have been XH538 ex-No. 230 OCU. This Vulcan was allocated to the Scampton Wing on 14 May 1969 after receiving a manufacturer's retrofit, although it left shortly afterwards for further modifications (27 June–20 August 1969) before rejoining the Wing. This aircraft would then have been available for the training of aircrew in the conventional bombing role. The process of converting all of the Blue Steel aircraft back to free-fall bombing would take just over two years, with approximately four to five Vulcans passing through the system at any one point in time. It was 10 November 1971 before the last of these aircraft XL427 returned to service with No. 27 Sqn.

Before the end of 1969 six Vulcans had returned to Scampton after conversion and it would have been these aircraft, along with XH538, in which the crews of No. 27 Sqn trained in order to become operational in the new year (XL318, XL320, XL361, XL386, XL426 and XM575). Now that there were only two squadrons stationed at Scampton, both operating in different roles, squadron markings began to reappear on individual aircraft. No. 617 Sqn adopted three red (day-glow) lightning flashes and No. 27 Sqn displayed a red (day-glow) elephant representing the cartoon character Dumbo. At least three aircraft were noted to have the day-glow elephant on their tail fin (XL318, XL361 and XM574). The latter aircraft became the eighth to be reconverted and arrived back at Scampton on 30 January 1970 (XM595 was the seventh, arriving on 14 January). These markings appear to indicate that after reconversion the previously mentioned Vulcans were more than likely those used by No. 27 Sqn in order to become operational in the new year. XL318 also displayed the same marking on the crew entrance door. In 1971 the Dumbo elephant was applied to the squadron's aircraft in a more colourful form placed on a white circular background. Although No. 230 OCU moved into Scampton from Finningley in December 1969, its aircraft remained outside the assignment of the Scampton Wing.

From August 1969 until the disbandment of No. 27 Sqn on 29 March

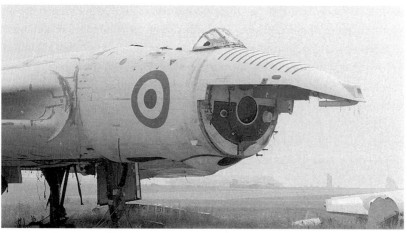

Figure 7.2:
Having first flown in August 1958, XH533 served for over eleven years with the A&AEE and was used to conduct numerous trials. The aircraft is shown at the end of its career at RAF St Athan in 1970 before being scrapped. Notice the additional pitot heads on the port side of the nose, also the fairing at the tip of the nose.
(Colin J. Dodds)

1972 there were twenty-five Vulcans used by the two Scampton squadrons. The aircraft concerned were XH538, XL317–21, XL359–61, XL384, XL386–90, XL392, XL425–7, XL443, XL444, XM574, XM575, XM594 and XM595. Close inspection of these serial numbers show that only four 'XL' aircraft are absent. XL385 had been written off in a ground accident in 1967, XL446 was operating with the OCU and XL391 along with XL445 were both allocated to the NEAF in Cyprus. The next thing to note is that the first five production 'XM' serial Vulcans with Olympus 201 engines, XM569–73, were also operating in Cyprus with the NEAF at that time. XH538 transferred to the Waddington Wing on 29 April 1970.

After being reconverted and then returned to service at Scampton some of the aircraft remained devoid of squadron markings and are recorded as being allocated to the Scampton Wing, as opposed to an individual squadron. These aircraft would have been used by both squadrons, allowing No. 617 Sqn to begin training some of its aircrew in their intended new

(See colour Plate 3)

role (reverting to free-fall bombing in the new year) prior to flying the final Blue Steel sortie on 21 December 1970. Some of the aircraft noted displaying No. 617 Sqn's markings (lightening flashes) on the tail fin were XL321, XL360, XL387, XL390, XL427 and XL443. Whilst still operating in the Blue Steel role in 1969, XL361 displayed three smaller red (day-glow) lightening flashes with the number '617' painted in the same colour beneath them. During 1971 No. 27 Sqn applied the new Dumbo insignia to its aircraft. Three of the Vulcans known to have displayed this marking at that time were XL443, XM574 and XM595. In 1971 No. 617 Sqn also introduced a far more colourful badge on to its Vulcans, which depicted three red lightening flashes above a yellow breeched dam with water flowing through and placed on a white diamond background edged in blue. One of the earlier aircraft displaying the new markings was XL317 noted in September 1971.

Figure 7.3:
Having recently been reconverted to conventional bombing standard, after serving for over eight years in the Blue Steel role, XL443 is seen during a display at Plymouth in about June/July 1971. Just visible on the tail fin is the upper part of No. 27 Sqn's insignia (Dumbo the elephant on a white circular background).
(Colin J. Dodds)

On 1 April 1970 XL386 left the assignment of the Scampton Wing to join No. 230 OCU. This was followed by XL319 on 14 May, having returned to Scampton from Woodford (manufacturer's modifications completed on the 28th) on the last day of April. XL319 was then loaned to the Scampton Wing on 12 November 1970 for a day only. Two further aircraft had also joined the OCU by the end of the year (XL361 and XL384). By the time No. 617 Sqn had flown its final Blue Steel sortie there were only six aircraft remaining in service waiting to be reconverted: XL317, XL321, XL360, XL387, XL427 and XL443. Together with the previously mentioned six aircraft, there were thirteen other Vulcan B.Mk2s operating with the two Scampton squadrons at that time (December 1970): XL318, XL320, XL359, XL388–90, XL392, XL425, XL426, XM574, XM575, XM594 and XM595. This allocation of nineteen would have allowed for eight aircraft each and three spare. Only one of Scampton's Vulcans was away at

that time receiving manufacturer's modifications at Bitteswell (XL444 27 August–31 December 1970). A further aircraft (XL392) had by then returned to service after having been away for manufacturer's modifications (reconversion) from 25 June to 13 November 1970.

During 1971 both XL360 and XL359 transferred over to the OCU (13 July and 21 October respectively) where they remained for the foreseeable future. On 22 April 1971 XL319 was transferred from the OCU to No. 617 Sqn until May 1972. From 10 May 1971 to 28 January 1972, XL388 is recorded as operating jointly with the Scampton Wing and the OCU. XL320, XL321, XL359, XL390, XL392, XL426, XL427 and XL444, together with the three previously mentioned aircraft, XL443, XM574 and XM595 (Dumbo elephant marking), are all understood to have been allocated to No. 27 Sqn for varying periods during 1971. On 27 July 1971 Prince Charles took a flight in XL392 whilst it displayed No. 617 Sqn's crest on the crew entrance door. His Captain for the flight was Flt Lt Peter Perry.

On 3 November 1971 XM574 of No. 27 Sqn was transferred to the Waddington Wing for twenty-one months, before joining the NEAF Bomber Wing in August 1973. By the end of 1971 all of the aircraft were now converted and operating in the free-fall bombing role. Taking into account the transfer of several aircraft to the OCU, along with the allocation of XM574 to the Waddington Wing, meant that there were sixteen Vulcans remaining with the two squadrons. No. 27 Sqn would continue to serve for the first three months of 1972 before disbanding on 29 March. It was on that very day that three of the squadron's Vulcans were allocated to No. 230 OCU (XL320, XL321 and XL426). On the same day one of the Scampton Wing's Olympus 301 series Vulcans (XM594) departed

Figure 7.4:
XM595 displaying the 'Dumbo' insignia on the tail fin whilst on static display at RAF Alconbury on 14 August 1971. Notice the aircraft's serial number repeated on the undercarriage doors and the small (coolant) blister under the wing (above the main undercarriage door). (APN)

its home base, were it had served for the past nine years, to head for the manufacturer's facilities to receive further modifications. After the completion of this work XM594 joined the Waddington Wing where it was destined to remain for the next ten years. Also in March another of the squadron's aircraft, XL392, was selected to conduct further trials on the Olympus 201 engines in an attempt to reduce the smoke emissions. These trials were the second in a series, with the first trial allegedly conducted in 1971 by XH558 of the Waddington Wing. No. 27 Sqn reformed in November 1973 operating in a different role and is described in a separate Chapter.

During the four months that followed after the disbandment of No. 27 Sqn more of the ex-Blue Steel aircraft were allocated to other Units. The first of these occurred on 7 April 1972 when XL389 of No. 617 Sqn moved to the OCU, although this Vulcan did return to its parent Unit on 30 June 1972. The second movement took place on 12 April 1972 when XL443 (ex-No. 27 Sqn) was flown to Cyprus to join the NEAF. Two more Vulcans were transferred to the OCU starting with XL318 on 22 May followed by XL319, which firstly received manufacturer's modifications at Woodford (8 May–19 September 1972) before returning to Scampton to join the OCU on 21 September 1972. Also in May XL425 left Scampton for six months (17 May–30 November 1972) to receive further manufacturer's modifications. After the completion of the work XL425 was allocated to No. 617 Sqn where the appropriate squadron markings were applied to the tail fin. After serving with No. 27 Sqn during 1971/72 (apart from an absence for manufacturer's modifications 17 June–10 November 1971) XL427 of the Scampton Wing transferred to the OCU for a week commencing 29 June, before being allocated to No. 617 Sqn on 5 July 1972. XL427 remained with it for about twelve weeks before returning to the OCU on 25 September 1972. On the same day as XL427 transferred from the OCU to No. 617 Sqn (5 July), XL387 made the reverse journey to join the OCU.

Throughout September and October 1972 there were only seven aircraft allocated to No. 617 Sqn. This probably explains why XL388 along with XL321 of the OCU was attached to No. 617 Sqn for a short period during those two months (XL388, September and XL321, October) in order to maintain the squadron's strength of eight Vulcans.

In November 1972 when XL425 arrived back at Scampton after receiving manufacturer's modifications, No. 617 Sqn was operating four Olympus 201 series aircraft (XL317, XL425, XL426 and XL444) along with four 301 series aircraft (XL389, XL390, XM575 and XM595). In addition to these eight aircraft XL392, which after the completion of the previously mentioned engine trials, is recorded as being allocated to the Scampton Wing. This would have allowed for one spare aircraft at that time.

Working in conjunction with No. 230 OCU, but given the task of training the Vulcan's rear crew in the use of the H2S radar, were the Hastings T.Mk5s of the Strike Command Bombing School. This Unit had been operating its ten aircraft from RAF Lindholme in Yorkshire through-out the 1960s. The Unit, which was unofficially known as '1066' Sqn, moved its remaining Hastings into RAF Scampton when Lindholme closed (1 September 1972). At that point in time there was only No. 230 OCU and No. 617 Sqn stationed there. Throughout 1973 the Hastings shared the airfield with twenty-three Vulcan B.Mk2s operated by the two resident Units (XH538, XH554, XH559, XL317–21, XL359–61, XL386–90, XL392, XL425–7, XL444, XM575 and XM595). Naturally a percentage of these Vulcans would have been out of service at any one time receiving manufacturer's modifications, e.g. (XL318, October 1972–April 1973 and XL426, July 1973–February 1974). However, XL387 of No. 230 OCU remained at Scampton for the first ten days of 1973 before being trans-ferred to the Waddington Wing on 10 January, were it remained for the next nine years.

On 17 December 1973 the resident Vulcans were joined by the arrival of XH563, which became the first B.Mk2 MRR delivered to No. 27 Sqn, recently reformed on 1 November 1973. Until further B.Mk2 MRRs became available a number of Scampton's resident Vulcans were loaned to No. 27 Sqn. XL425 became the first B.Mk2 loaned to it from No. 617 Sqn for five months (1 November 1973–1 April 1974). No. 230 OCU loaned XL388 to No. 617 Sqn for 'exactly' the same period in order for that squadron to maintain its numbers. No. 230 OCU had sufficient Vulcans on strength at the end of March 1974, so when XL425 returned to reclaim its slot with No. 617 Sqn (1 April 1974), the 301 series Vulcan, XL388, transferred to the Waddington Wing. No. 617 Sqn transferred another of its 301 series Vulcans (XL389) to the Waddington Wing on 6 June 1974. After the transfer of XL388 and XL389, No. 617 Sqn only had six aircraft allocated to it (XL317, XL390, XL392, XL425, XL426 and XL444) as XM595 was out of service receiving manufacturer's modifica-tions (11 February–16 August 1974). Until the squadron received more aircraft of its own, No. 617 Sqn made occasional use of the OCU's air-craft. One example of this was XL319 being used by No. 617 Sqn on 3 May 1974. No. 617 Sqn gained an additional aircraft on 14 January 1975 when XL361 joined the squadron after transferring from the OCU. XL361 had been operating with the MOD (PE) at the A&AEE during the second half of December 1974. The same aircraft was loaned to this Unit later in the year for about a month (7 August–3 September 1975) before returning to No. 617 Sqn.

Two days after XL361 joined No. 617 Sqn in January 1975, No. 35 Sqn returned to the UK from Cyprus and was to be stationed at Scampton. The first four of its aircraft arrived at Scampton on the 16th followed by the remaining four Vulcans on 24 January 1975. It was one of the Vulcans in the second wave (XM574) that transferred to No. 617 Sqn on 14 August 1975. The following month XM595, which had been serving with No. 27 Sqn after receiving its manufacturer's modifications in 1974, rejoined No. 617 Sqn in September 1975. At that time XL390, which still displayed the red/white/blue national markings, was at Bitteswell receiving manufacturer's modifications (6 February–3 October 1975). This left the squadron in September 1975 with an allocation of eight Vulcans: XL317, XL361, XL392, XL425, XL426, XL444, XM574 and XM595.

Over the past few years the colour schemes on the Vulcans began to change. Among the changes was the introduction of low-visibility national markings (red/blue), along with 'light aircraft grey' painted on the aircraft's underside and an overall matt finish replacing the previous glossy coating. Prior to being completely repainted, some of the Vulcans received only the red and blue national markings. During the following years further changes took place with the grey camouflage being extended over the black radome and the introduction of the passive ECM (radar warning receiver) fitted to the top of the aircraft's tail fin.

One month after XL390 had returned to No. 617 Sqn (now fitted with the radar warning receiver on its tail) another of the squadron's aircraft, XL317, departed to Bitteswell to receive further manufacturer's modifications (10 November 1975–18 October 1976). For seven months after the departure of XL317 the squadron operated the following eight aircraft: XL361, XL390, XL392, XL425, XL426, XL444, XM574 and XM595. It was then the turn of XL392 to leave Scampton for Bitteswell to receive its manufacturer's modifications (21 May 1976–25 February 1977). In August 1976 XL444 appeared at the Greenham Common Open Day, having not yet received its passive ECM tail fin. XL444 continued to serve with the squadron until 25 January 1977, before taking its turn at Bitteswell for ten months returning to No. 617 Sqn on 17 November 1977. It would probably have been the same aircrew that returned XL444 to Scampton that delivered XL426 to Bitteswell on the same day to begin its modifications (17 November 1977–21 June 1978). XL444 remained with No. 617 Sqn until 31 May 1978 when it then transferred to No. 35 Sqn. For virtually the same period that XL444 last served with No. 617 Sqn (17 November 1977–31 May 1978) and XL426 received its modifications (17 November

1977–21 June 1978), the squadron operated XL360 (5 December 1977–31 May 1978). XL360 was an ex-OCU aircraft that had just returned to service after the completion of its manufacturer's modifications. This Vulcan then transferred to No. 35 Sqn.

In July 1977 the surviving Hastings T.Mk5s, which were being operated by the Hastings Radar Flight, were retired (displayed No. 230 OCU insignia on tail fin). The Hastings Radar Flight had originally formed on 1 January 1974 after the previous Strike Command Bombing School disbanded.

On 8 August 1977 XL361 was transferred to No. 35 Sqn, having served with No. 617 Sqn for the past two-and-a-half years. This aircraft could be distinguished from all of the other Vulcans on the squadron because it had two small white-blade aerials on the top of its nose, similar to the B.Mk2 MRRs of No. 27 Sqn. Both of the bomber squadrons at Scampton (Nos 35 and 617) had a secondary role of MRR assigned to them in order to give assistance to No. 27 Sqn in times of emergency. Another of No. 617 Sqn's aircraft is recorded as being operated by No. 35 Sqn from November 1976 to February 1978, although this Vulcan (XM595) was known to be still wearing No. 617 Sqn's insignia in August 1977.

When XM595 was allocated back to No. 617 Sqn in February 1978 it shared the squadron's dispersals with XL317, XL360, XL390, XL392, XL425, XL444 and XM574. The squadron operated these eight Vulcans until the end of May 1978 when, as previously mentioned, XL360 and XL444 transferred to No. 35 Sqn. For the next three weeks until the return of XL426 (21 June 1978) the squadron had only six aircraft allocated to it.

Figure 7.5: XL426 of No. 617 Sqn, parked on the squadron's dispersal at Scampton in August 1977. Notice that the aircraft has yet to receive the passive ECM on the top of its tail fin. (Author's collection)

Figure 7.6:
*XL390 of No. 617
Sqn at RAF
Leeming's Open Day
on 23 April 1978.
This aircraft was due
to give a flying dis-
play but remained on
the ground due to a
technical fault.*
(Author's collection)

On 23 April 1978 XL390 of No. 617 Sqn appeared at the RAF Leeming Open Day, positioned on the station's main apron adjacent to the static park. Later in the day it was to carry out its flying display, so in the mean time the crowds waited anxiously. When the time came the aircraft moved forward for a short distance and then paused. After a further period of waiting by the spectators an announcement came over the speakers, 'I am sorry to announce … that due to a technical fault the Vulcan will not be flying today, sorry.' XL390 did participate in a flying display during April 1978 when it led a formation of aircraft (Jaguar, Canberra and Buccaneer) to mark the tenth anniversary of Strike Command. Three-and-a-half months later XL390 was in the USA at the same time that four other Vulcans were participating in the 1978 'Giant Voice' bombing competition. On 12 August 1978 whilst practising for an air display XL390 failed to recover from a wing over and crashed with the loss of all the crew near to Glenview Naval Air Station.

At the time of the crash XL446 of No. 35 Sqn was operating with the Waddington Wing. On 31 October 1978 when this aircraft returned to Scampton, it was allocated to No. 617 Sqn. In the meantime No. 35 Sqn loaned XM570 to No. 617 Sqn as a temporary aircraft for eight weeks (4 September–31 October 1978) until substituted by XL446. On 23 November 1978 No. 617 Sqn received a further ex-No. 35 Sqn Vulcan when XJ783 arrived at Scampton from Bitteswell having just completed its modification work. This Vulcan was the only 'XJ' serial aircraft that No. 617 Sqn operated. It was also the only one operated by it over the past seventeen years with the twin Skybolt blisters under its wings. By the end

Figure 7.7:
With the undercarriage down, the air brakes out and the nose held high, XL425 of No. 617 Sqn comes in to land after completing its display at Prestwick on 27 June 1979.
(John Huggon)

of 1978 the squadron was operating XJ783, XL317, XL392, XL425, XL426, XL446, XM574 and XM595.

On 9 January 1979 XM571 of No. 35 Sqn went to St Athan for a major service and a new coat of paint. When the work was completed the aircraft joined No. 617 Sqn at Scampton (27 March 1979). For four months beginning 20 August, XM571 operated with the Waddington Wing before returning to No. 617 Sqn. It was during November 1979 that XM571 participated in the 'Giant Voice' bombing competition at Barksdale AFB, Louisiana. Together with XL387, XM571 went on to compete in the final phase of the competition. Whilst at Barksdale AFB, the words 'GRANNY BASHER' were painted in red (day-glow) on the starboard side nose wheel door (XM571). To the right of this there was a large 'club' protruding from a small RAF roundel poised ready to strike a character

(See colour Plate 4)

Figure 7.8:
Whilst deployed to RAF Leeming on 16 October 1979, XL426 is kept under guard. Notice the air–oil separator pipes between the two port engines and the ECM equipment bay-cooling 'intake' on the starboard side of the rear fuselage. The latter fitting was present on all B.Mk2s but was removed from the six aircraft converted to K.Mk2 standard.
(Author's collection)

Figure 7.9:
A crew from No. 617 Sqn, flying XL446, carry out a practice approach followed by a touch-and-go at RAF Finningley on 20–26 June 1979.
(CBV)

wearing a pointed hat. On 4 December 1979 this aircraft returned to No. 617 Sqn at Scampton. The squadron operated these nine Vulcans until XJ783 returned to No. 35 Sqn on 3 April 1981.

In December 1979 XL426 operated from Nellis AFB in the USA as a participant in the realistic American training exercise known as Red Flag. The aircraft was one of four Vulcans (XL361 No. 35 Sqn, XM652 No. 44 Sqn displaying the new wrap-round camouflage and XM612 No. 101 Sqn) taking part in the exercise that involved flying low-level sorties over the rugged terrain at night. This was the second occasion out of the three Red Flag exercises where the RAF Vulcans participated in night-time sorties. Faced with the multiple air and ground threats, the Vulcan crews proved the critics wrong by penetrating through the defence screens undetected and destroyed their targets. One way to sum up this performance is 'Red Flag at night, Vulcan's delight.' XL426 had participated in 'Red Flag 1978' along with XL444 of No. 35 Sqn, XM612 of No. 50 Sqn and XM657 of No. 44 Sqn.

During 1981 two of the squadron's Vulcans, XL425 and XL426, received the new wrap-round camouflage scheme whilst being serviced at St Athan. The latter aircraft became the 298th and last Vulcan to receive a major service at St Athan (4 February–21 May 1981). On 1 July 1981 XL318 of No. 230 OCU (wrap-round camouflage) came back to serve once again with the 'Dambusters'. XL318 was the first B.Mk2 delivered to No. 617 Sqn on 4 September 1961. In 1981 the Vulcan's service life was coming to an end and its role within NATO would eventually be handed over to the Tornado. The first casualty was to be the Vulcan OCU that disbanded on 31 August 1981. On that very same day XM574 of No. 617 Sqn ended its service when it was flown to St Athan for salvage and eventually scrapped in January 1982.

The squadron continued to operate its remaining eight Vulcans (XL317, XL318, XL392, XL425, XL426, XL446, XM571 and XM595) until December 1981. With only one month remaining before the RAF's most famous bomber squadron disbanded, plans were made for the disposal of its aircraft. XL317 became the first one to leave the squadron with which it had served for twenty years, and was flown to Akrotiri in Cyprus (1 December 1981) to be allocated for crash rescue training on the station's dump. Included in the crew of XL317 on its final flight was RAF Scampton's Station Commander. This aircraft survived for a further five years before being scrapped in 1986 (displayed No. 35 Sqn markings together with several other RAF squadrons, e.g. No. 92 Sqn). Ten days after XL317 made its final flight, XL318 carried out No. 617 Sqn's final Vulcan sortie on 11 December 1981. During the flight the aircraft made a low-level pass over the Derwent Reservoir/Dam in the Peak District near Sheffield. This was one of the locations where the squadron's Lancaster Bombers, with their famous bouncing bombs, trained during 1943 in preparation for the Dambuster raids under the command of Wg Cdr Guy Gibson. After returning to Scampton XL318's engines were shut down for the final time.

On 31 December 1981 No. 617 Sqn disbanded and after the new year three of its Vulcans, XL392, XL446 and XM595, were allocated to No. 35 Sqn on 4 January 1982. On the same day XL425 was declared CAT 5C and later scrapped on site, whilst XL318 was assigned for preservation at the RAF Museum at Hendon. The aircraft was dismantled at Scampton and then transported by road to the Museum (19 February–5 March 1982). On 5 January 1982 XL426 joined No. 50 Sqn at Waddington, followed by XM571 on 8 January that joined No. 101 Sqn.

No. 617 Sqn reformed at RAF Marham on 16 May 1983 equipped with Tornado GR.Mk1s.

Returning to January 1975, No. 35 Sqn had arrived at Scampton from Akrotiri in Cyprus, to what would now become its fourth base in just twelve years whilst operating the Vulcan Bomber. The squadron's eight aircraft arrived in two groups of four on separate days (16 January: XJ783, XJ825, XL445, XL446; 24th: XJ824, XL443, XM572, XM574). On 6 March XH561 (ex-NEAF) arrived at Scampton having just received its manufacturer's modifications during the previous eleven months. After being allocated this additional aircraft, No. 35 Sqn was now in a position to release XJ825, which made the reverse journey to Bitteswell the following day

Figure 7.10:
Whilst conducting a display at Prestwick on 14 June 1975, XM571 is seen displaying No. 35 Sqn's insignia on the tail fin. The tip of the blade aerial positioned on the starboard ECM plate is below the aircraft's tail.
(John Huggon)

(manufacturer's modifications, 7 March 1975–13 January 1976). Prior to No. 35 Sqn returning to the UK, XM571 of the NEAF had been allocated to No. 27 Sqn at Scampton as a standard B.Mk2 (1 January 1975). Fourteen weeks later XM571 rejoined No. 35 Sqn (9 April 1975). At about this time No. 35 Sqn had began to apply markings onto the tail fin of all its aircraft, depicting the squadron number '35' (both numbers being entangled) painted in yellow (XL445 is understood to have initially displayed the Unit's 'winged horse'). Beginning on 5 June 1975, XJ824 received modifications at Bitteswell before returning to the squadron on 26 February 1976. During the time that XJ824 was away for modifications, XM571 had been loaned to the Waddington Wing for about five months (18 June–3 November 1975) and XM574 was transferred to No. 617 Sqn on 14 August 1975. At the end of January 1976 No. 35 Sqn had been back in the UK for a year, its allocation of Vulcan B.Mk2s at that point was: XH561, XJ783, XJ825, XL443, XL445, XL446, XM571 and XM572.

After the return of XJ824 to No. 35 Sqn in February 1976 its total increased to nine, but this number decreased (15 June 1976) when XM571 was once again allocated to the Waddington Wing. During July 1976 No. 50 Sqn's insignia was applied to XM571's tail fin. The aircraft remained with No. 50 Sqn until being returning to No. 35 Sqn on 15 November 1976. During the winter months there were a number of changes within No. 35 Sqn with the transfer of XM570 from No. 27 Sqn on 8 October 1976 in exchange for XJ825 a week later (15th). This was followed by the departure of XM572 to Bitteswell on 27 October to receive manufacturer's modifications (completed ten months later on 23 August 1977). The next move occurred on 14 February 1977 when XJ824 was transferred to No. 230 OCU, followed a fortnight later by the temporary loan to the

OCU of XM570 (28 February–2 March 1977). On 28 March XM571 was flown to Bitteswell to receive manufacturer's modifications, which were completed on 17 April 1978. By April 1977 the aircraft allocated to the squadron were: XH561, XJ783, XL443, XL445, XL446 and XM570. No. 35 Sqn made use of an additional aircraft from No. 617 Sqn (XM595) throughout 1977 to help maintain numbers. XM595 is shown to have operated with No. 35 Sqn from November 1976 to February 1978 and it is understood to have retained the insignia of its parent Unit (No. 617 Sqn) for some time throughout that period. XH559 of No. 230 OCU was also seen in 1977 displaying the markings of No. 35 Sqn when it appeared at RAF Finningley at the end of July. This aircraft presumably operated with the squadron to increase its number to eight Vulcans, although it is recorded as remaining with the OCU at that time. At the same time No. 230 OCU had ten aircraft allocated to it, so would therefore have been able to cope quite well with the absence of XH559. The markings displayed on this aircraft were more predominant to those described earlier as they now had the original '35' badge placed on a dark green oval background outlined in yellow. All of the squadron's aircraft now displayed the more predominant insignia, although only a few had the rectangular ECM fairing at the top of the tail fin, e.g. XJ825, XH559 and XM571.

During July and August No. 35 Sqn received two additional aircraft in the form of XH538 on 28 July 1977 (ex-OCU, returning from manufacturer's modifications) and XL361 transferring from No. 617 Sqn on 3 August 1977. Twenty days later XM572 rejoined the squadron after returning from Bitteswell on 23 August 1977. Meanwhile XL445 had been

Figure 7.11: *Representing No. 35 Sqn during the Queen's Jubilee celebrations at RAF Finningley on 29/30 July 1977 was XH559. Although this aircraft has always lacked the Terrain-Following Radar it is equipped (about mid-1970s) with the single-emitter head version of the 'X band jammer' under the rear fuselage.*
(John Huggon)

Craig Bulman

attached to the Waddington Wing for three-and-a-half months from 16 June to 1 October 1977. By the end of August 1977 No. 35 Sqn was operating the following nine aircraft: XH538, XH561, XJ783, XL361, XL443, XL446, XM570, XM572 and XM595 (the latter aircraft still wearing No. 617 Sqn markings). On 7 September 1977 it was the turn of XL446 to go across to Bitteswell for manufacturer's modifications. This aircraft returned to No. 35 Sqn on 10 May 1978 for two weeks before operating with the Waddington Wing for the next five months, but still displaying the markings of its parent squadron. The day before XL446 returned from Bitteswell, XL443 was delivered there from Scampton to begin its modification work (9 May 1978) that took until 5 February 1979 to complete. XJ783 was also at Bitteswell at that time to receive similar modifications (7 March–23 November 1978). Both XJ783 and XL443 were joined by XL361, which arrived at Bitteswell on 5 September 1978. XL361 returned to No. 35 Sqn on 6 July 1979, unlike XJ783 which was issued to No. 617 Sqn after completion of the work.

Two former No. 617 Sqn Vulcans XL360 and XL444 transferred to No. 35 Sqn on 31 May 1978 to join the seven aircraft already allocated to it (XH538, XH561, XL361, XL445, XM570, XM571 and XM572). On 16 August 1978 XH538 (ex-Skybolt test aircraft) transferred to the Waddington Wing until 23 November 1979. On 16 October 1978 No. 230 OCU exchanged XL319 for XL445 of No. 35 Sqn. XL319 was now destined to remain with the squadron until its disbandment in February 1982, apart from a visit to Bitteswell for modifications (22 May 1979–25 March 1980). One other movement took place during 1978 (shortly after the loss of XL390 in the USA) when XM570 was loaned to No. 617 Sqn for eight weeks from 4 September to 31 October 1978. By the end of 1978 the

Figure 7.12:
Five Vulcan B.Mk2s of No. 35 Sqn sit silently on their dispersals at Scampton in August 1977 (XH538, XH561, XL361, XL443 and XM570, all equipped with the 'passive ECM' tail fin). Notice the exhaust covers in place on the two nearest aircraft.
(Author's collection)

squadron's allocation of Vulcan B.Mk2s consisted of XH561, XL319, XL360, XL444, XM570, XM571 and XM572. In late 1978 XL444 was flown to Nellis AFB, Nevada to participate in Red Flag.

Early in the new year XM571 departed for St Athan to receive a major service and upon return was then issued to No. 617 Sqn (9 January–27 March 1979). Experience gained by the Vulcan detachments during the participation in Red Flag showed a need for a colour scheme change. In September 1979 XM652 of No. 44 Sqn became the first Vulcan to receive the new wrap-round camouflage. No. 35 Sqn received its first similar camouflaged Vulcan in December 1979 when XH561 returned from St Athan having just had a major service. By the end of 1979 the eight aircraft on strength were XH538, XH561, XL360, XL361, XL443, XL444, XM570 and XM572 (XL361 participated in Red Flag in December). With the exception of XH561, which received manufacturer's modifications at Bitteswell during 1980 (14 March 1980–6 February 1981), No. 35 Sqn continued to operate the remaining seven aircraft throughout the year. Along with XL319, which returned to the squadron in March, a further Vulcan XH562 (ex-OCU) joined No. 35 Sqn on 16 December 1980.

As 1981 approached, the Vulcan Force was entering its final phase and the planned run-down of the Scampton Wing Units would begin shortly. No. 230 OCU was earmarked to disband in August 1981 followed by No. 617 Sqn at the end of the year, preceding Nos 27 and 35 Sqns in early 1982.

At the beginning of February 1981 XH561 returned from Bitteswell increasing the squadron's allocation to ten (XH538, XH561, XH562, XL319, XL360, XL361, XL443, XL444, XM570 and XM572). On 11 March 1981 two of the squadron's Vulcans (XH538 and XM570) were flown to St Athan and declared CAT 5C for the salvage of useful components (scrapped August 1981 and January 1982 respectively). Although these two Vulcans certainly had a good innings, this was an undignified ending to two superb aircraft. During April two further aircraft left the squadron, however three other Vulcans came along and increased the squadron's total to nine. These movements began with the transfer of XJ823 from No. 27 Sqn on 2 April 1981 (No. 35 Sqn's first ever Vulcan B.Mk2 in January 1963). This transfer occurred exactly one year before the Argentine invasion of the Falkland Islands. The next day XJ783 transferred from No. 617 Sqn back to No. 35 Sqn (3 April 1981). Further movements occurred on 6 April when XJ825 (ex-No. 27 Sqn) transferred to No. 35 Sqn and XL444 left for Waddington where it joined No. 9 Sqn the following month. One week later (13 April) XL361 was also transferred to the Waddington Wing. This aircraft retained its No. 35 Sqn markings until June, when it then received No. 9 Sqn's insignia. The next move occurred on 19 June when XH562 followed XL361 and XL444 by firstly transferring to the Waddington Wing and then being allocated to No. 9 Sqn (July 1981).

Pending the disbandment of the OCU in August, three of its aircraft, XL321, XL359 and XL445, were transferred to No. 35 Sqn on 1 July 1981 (the latter two Vulcans were painted in the wrap-round camouflage scheme). By August 1981 No. 35 Sqn was operating the following eleven aircraft: XH561, XJ783, XJ823, XJ825, XL319, XL321, XL359, XL360, XL443, XL445 and XM572.

The Waddington Wing was to receive two more of No. 35 Sqn's Vulcans in September, when XM572 joined No. 9 Sqn on the 2nd and XH561 joined No. 50 Sqn on the 4th. XL321 was used by No. 617 Sqn for three weeks (14 September–6 October 1981) before continuing with No. 35 Sqn. The next Vulcan to leave the squadron was XL445 on 18 November when it transferred to No. 44 Sqn at Waddington. By the end of the year, with just under two months remaining, No. 35 Sqn operated the following eight aircraft: XJ783, XJ823, XJ825, XL319, XL321, XL359, XL360 and XL443, but the story does not end there …

Four days after the disbandment of No. 617 Sqn (31 December 1981) marked the arrival of three further aircraft, XL392, XL446 and XM595, from the Dambusters to No. 35 Sqn (4 January 1982). On the same day XL443 was withdrawn from service. Initially this aircraft had been earmarked for preservation at the RAF Museum, but this was changed to XL318 of No. 617 Sqn. XL443 then met with the fate of being declared CAT 5C and eventually scrapped. The day after the three ex-No. 617 Sqn aircraft joined No. 35 Sqn, XL360 was allocated to No. 101 Sqn at

Figure 7.13:
XJ783 coming in to land on runway 23 at Scampton at some time during its final tour of duty with No. 35 Sqn (April 1981–February 1982), Notice the darker grey 'triangular' patch directly above the squadron's insignia, indicating the location of its previous Unit's insignia, No. 617 Sqn. **(CBV)**

Waddington. Although this aircraft had been re-allocated in January it was still parked on No. 35 Sqn's dispersals at Scampton, displaying its intended new owner's insignia and the Lincoln coat of arms until at least 20 March 1982. On 21 January 1982 XL321 joined No. 50 Sqn at Waddington. This left No. 35 Sqn with eight aircraft to operate during the final month of service, before disbanding on 26 February 1982: XJ783, XJ823, XJ825, XL319, XL359, XL392, XL446 and XM595. By the end of the month this well-known bomber squadron was to be stood down to take its place in the history books.

With the exception of XL392, which was flown to RAF Valley and placed onto the fire dump for crash rescue training (24 March 1982), all of the remaining Vulcans on the squadron had their futures or fates allocated to them on 1 March 1982. Initially XL359 had been earmarked for preservation as Scampton's gate guard (changed to XH563), but instead it was placed onto the station's dump for a while before being scrapped on site (November 1982). Three more of the Vulcans, XJ783, XL446 and XM595, were declared CAT 5C at Scampton and also later scrapped. The three surviving aircraft were more fortunate as they were transferred to Waddington to continue in service with the remaining bomber squadrons. XJ823 arrived at Waddington where the previous squadron's insignia was replaced by the letter 'C' painted in orange (significance unknown). This aircraft had been noted with this marking at Waddington on 20 March 1982. XJ823 was taken into one of the station's hangars on 1 April 1982 and when it re-emerged it displayed No. 50 Sqn's insignia. The remaining two Vulcans, XJ825 and XL319, were both displaying the Lincoln coat of arms along with their new squadron insignia in March 1982 (Nos 101 and 44 Sqns respectively).

After the disbandment of No. 35 Sqn, the only Vulcans remaining in service at Scampton belonged to No. 27 Sqn. This squadron had been operating Vulcan B.Mk2s in a bombing/missile capacity from 1961 until disbandment in 1972. After a short period the squadron was reformed at Scampton operating in a different role.

Maritime Radar Reconnaissance

A T MIDNIGHT ON 30 JUNE 1969 the Royal Navy took over the country's nuclear deterrent role, with Polaris missile-equipped submarines. This left the RAF with a greatly reduced nuclear commitment and a surplus of nuclear bombers. On 29 March 1972 No. 27 Sqn at Scampton was disbanded. The squadron would not be out of action for long as it had been selected to take over the task currently carried out by the Victors of No. 543 Sqn at RAF Wyton. No. 27 Sqn would reform back at Scampton with modified versions of the Vulcan Bombers. The squadron's new role would be Maritime Radar Reconnaissance (MRR), with a secondary role of upper air sampling.

No. 27 Sqn reformed on 1 November 1973. The new version of the Vulcan would be known as the B.Mk2 MRR, sometimes referred to as SR.Mk2. The B.Mk2 MRR would have Loran C navigation equipment, a number of electronic sensors and some photographic equipment fitted to it. Owing to the nature of operations over the sea, there would be no requirement for the Terrain-Following Radar fitted to the aircraft's nose. The Vulcans would retain their glossy camouflage and have provisions to mount the under-wing pylons to carry the air-sampling pods. The first B.Mk2 MRRs were not yet ready to enter service, so the squadron was issued with a standard B.Mk2 on 1 November 1973. Transferring to the newly reformed squadron from the resident No. 617 Sqn was XL425. There would naturally be a period required for crew training before No. 27 Sqn actually carried out its first operational sortie. On 1 November when XL425 transferred to No. 27 Sqn, the vacant slot on No. 617 Sqn was immediately filled by XL388, which came across from No. 230 OCU on the same day (1 November 1973). One month later on 3 December, No. 27 Sqn received its second standard B.Mk2 in the form of XH538, which transferred from No. 230 OCU.

Across at Bitteswell in Leicestershire the first of the B.Mk2 MRR

Figure 8.1:
One of the additional pieces of equipment fitted to the B.Mk2 MRR was a camera positioned in the bomb-aiming fairing under the aircraft's nose as shown here in XH563.
(Terry Quinn)

version was nearing completion. This Vulcan (XH563) joined No. 27 Sqn on 17 December 1973, two weeks after the arrival of XH538. As XH563 departed on its delivery flight to Scampton, the vacant slot left behind at Bitteswell was immediately filled by XM654 arriving from Waddington for servicing and manufacturer's modifications. XM654 returned to the Waddington Wing (4 June 1974). After the arrival of XH563 in December, a further two weeks passed before the squadron's fourth aircraft arrived in the new year (4 January 1974). The Vulcan concerned was a further standard B.Mk2 XL427, which also transferred from No. 230 OCU.

In mid-January XL361 came from No. 230 OCU for additional crew training, but returned to the OCU a few days later (14–16 January 1974). The aircrew of No. 27 Sqn also operated XL318 of No. 230 OCU (31 January–1 February 1974). Throughout the second half of 1973 XL426 had been out of service for manufacturer's modifications. After the completion of the modifications the aircraft was issued to No. 27 Sqn, but remained with it for only two weeks (6–21 February 1974) before transferring to No. 617 Sqn.

From 17 January to 29 March 1974, No. 27 Sqn flew XL361 of No. 230 OCU about a dozen times. On 1 March 1974 XL361 flew No. 27 Sqn's first operational sortie. The sortie lasted five hours twenty minutes, taking the aircraft north to the Faeroe's Gap area of the Atlantic, where it was involved in a joint maritime exercise including fighter affiliation and attack support. One week after the squadron's first operational sortie, XM570 arrived at RAF Scampton (8 March 1974). XM570 (a standard B.Mk2) had been allocated to the squadron after serving the previous five years with the Near East Air Force Bomber Wing in Cyprus. A further week passed when the squadron received its second B.Mk2 MRR. XH560 arrived from Bitteswell after conversion and joined the squadron on 15 March 1974. The aircraft had been in storage (20 October 1971–1 February 1973) before its conversion.

On 1 April 1974 No. 27 Sqn's first Vulcan, XL425, returned to No. 617 Sqn. The next aircraft to join No. 27 Sqn was XM573, which also transferred from the NEAF Bomber Wing in Cyprus (17 April 1974). Six months had now passed since the reformation of the squadron. The current strength of Vulcans on the squadron was six: XH538, XL427, XM570, XM573 (standard B.Mk2s), XH560 and XH563 (B.Mk2 MRRs). The seventh Vulcan, a further B.Mk2 (XM569), joined No. 27 Sqn on 4 July 1974 after having served with the NEAF in Cyprus since 1969.

Squadron markings had been applied to these Vulcans, which showed an Indian elephant on a white circular background. At a later date these markings changed, displaying the cartoon character Dumbo. Close inspection of Dumbo would show two different markings, one wearing a small blue hat and the other goggles.

Three more Vulcans joined No. 27 Sqn during August and September 1974. XH534 a B.Mk2 MRR came along on 14 August 1974 after it had been in storage for sixteen months (7 March 1972–August 1973) prior to conversion. Two days later on 16 August 1974 XM595, a B.Mk2 with Olympus 301 engines returned from manufacturer's modifications to join

Figure 8.2:
XM573 was one of several standard B.Mk2s used by No. 27 Sqn until being replaced by additional B.Mk2 MRRs. This photo shows the aircraft (c.1975) displaying the insignia, which was initially used on the squadron's Vulcans, depicting an Indian elephant on a white circular background. Notice that the camouflage has been extended over the black radome. **(CBV)**

the squadron. At the USAF Alconbury Open Day in August 1971, XM595 was seen displaying No. 27 Sqn's Dumbo elephant markings on its tail fin. At that point the squadron was operating in the conventional/nuclear bombing role. On 17 September 1974 the fourth B.Mk2 MRR, XH558, arrived to join the squadron. For the remainder of 1974 there were ten Vulcans allocated to No. 27 Sqn, of which six were standard B.Mk2s.

On the third day of the new year XM571 of the NEAF became the first Vulcan B.Mk2 to be relocated in the UK after Turkish forces invaded the northern half of Cyprus (20 July 1974). XM571 served for three months with No. 27 Sqn before returning to No. 35 Sqn (9 April 1975), which was now also stationed at Scampton. On 15 January 1975 XH538 returned to the OCU after serving with No. 27 Sqn for about thirteen months. After the return of XM571 to No. 35 Sqn on 9 April the number of Vulcans on strength with No. 27 Sqn was nine. The aircraft were: XH534, XH558, XH560, XH563 (B.Mk2 MRRs), XL427, XM569, XM570, XM573 and XM595 (B.Mk2s). This number dropped to eight when XM595 returned to No. 617 Sqn in September 1975. During 1975 No. 27 Sqn continued to display the Indian elephant on its Vulcans. XH563 for example was at Scampton in May 1975 displaying these markings along with a black radome, red/blue roundels and a rectangular fairing at the fin-top. The following year Dumbo started to appear on more of the squadron's air-craft. These markings along with newly painted light and medium grey camouflaged radomes appeared on XH534 and XH560. XH558 was another squadron aircraft that had the Dumbo marking applied to it,

Figure 8.3:
Vulcan B.Mk2 MRR XH563 at Leuchars on 20 September 1975. Notice that the aircraft is equipped with the air-sampling pods mounted outboard and slightly to the rear of the twin Skybolt blisters. **(John Huggon)**

Craig Bulman

whilst retaining the red/white/blue roundels along with its white under-side that had been extended over the black radome (*c.*1975).

No. 27 Sqn continued throughout 1976 to operate these eight aircraft until November, when plans where about to be implemented to replace the four ex-Blue Steel Vulcans (XL427, XM569, XM570 and XM573), with more suitably equipped Vulcans. The replacements would also have Olympus 201 engines similar to all the current aircraft on the squadron and would come from earlier XH and XJ production batches that were partially converted for Skybolt in the 1960s. I wonder how the request sounded to members of the other Vulcan Units: 'Has anyone got an appropriate Vulcan they would like to swap with No. 27 Squadron?' On 23 November 1976 the first 'swap' (exchange) took place when XM569 flew the few miles south to Waddington and would soon be allocated to No. 9 Sqn, where the elephant on its fin would be replaced with a bat. On the same day XJ780 of No. 9 Sqn is recorded as transferring to No. 27 Sqn at Scampton. Just over a fortnight later on 8 December 1976 XM570 joined No. 35 Sqn at Scampton, and coming in the opposite direction was XJ825. This aircraft is recorded as joining No. 27 Sqn seven days later on 15 December 1976. It was several weeks before the next Vulcan of No. 27 Sqn was swapped, this time with one from No. 44 Sqn at Waddington. On 15 February 1977 XJ782, which had previously served with different Units at Scampton, Coningsby, Finningley, Waddington, Cottesmore and Akrotiri, left No. 44 Sqn and transferred to No. 27 Sqn, but records show that it was 9 March 1977 (about three weeks later) before XM573 trans-ferred the other way. The fourth swap came at the end of April 1977. XJ823 of No. 9 Sqn had been at St Athan in Wales since January 1977 receiving modifications to the (MRR) role before joining No. 27 Sqn on 27 April 1977. Five days later (2 May 1977) XL427 with its high-gloss colour scheme joined the Waddington Wing and was allocated to No. 9 Sqn. XL427 received the appropriate squadron markings and appeared at the Church Fenton Air Show the following month (June 1977) giving a magnificent display to the public, as always. This aircraft along with the previously mentioned XM573 appeared in the four-aircraft scramble at the Waddington Air Show (17 June 1978). The four Vulcans in the display were: XL427 No. 9 Sqn, XM573 No. 44 Sqn (both ex-No. 27 Sqn), XM654 No. 50 Sqn and XM605 No. 101 Sqn. For two years from April 1977 to April 1979 when XJ823 received a fresh coat of paint, the squadron's Dumbo elephant marking was displayed, but on close inspection of the tail fin the aircraft's previous operator's markings could be seen painted over in grey (No. 9 Sqn and the Lincoln coat of arms). The four new Vulcans on the squadron, XJ780, XJ782, XJ823 and XJ825 (all XJ), received

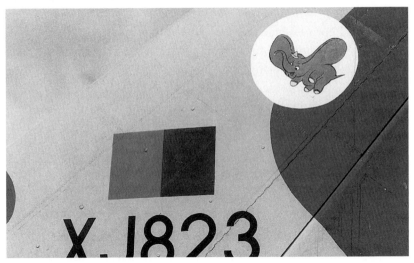

Figure 8.4:
The cartoon character Dumbo was adopted as the squadron's unofficial insignia, replacing the previous Indian elephant and is displayed here on the tail fin of XJ823.
(Author's collection)

Figure 8.5:
Vulcan B.Mk2 XL427 served with No. 27 Sqn at Scampton from 4 January 1974 until its transfer to No. 9 Sqn at Waddington on 2 May 1977. The aircraft is seen during a display at Church Fenton in June 1977 with the Lincoln coat of arms and the bat insignia of No. 9 Sqn (notice that the aircraft still has the glossy coating on the camouflage.
(Les Bulman)

Figure 8.6:
Having been modified to B.Mk2 MRR standard, XJ782 is shown back at Waddington whilst positioned on No. 44 Sqn's dispersal in August 1977 (it previously served with No. 44 Sqn until February 1977). By closely inspecting the top of the aircraft's nose, it is possible to see the white 'blade aerial' (a feature of the B.Mk2 MRR). Re Vulcan in the background is XM609 No. 44 Sqn.
(Author's collection)

similar modifications to the other B.Mk2 MRRs, XH534, XH558, XH560 and XH563, but lacked the additional under-wing fixings to carry the air-sampling pods and pylons. When not in use the pods and pylons were removed and then replaced by three small blisters, the forward two being slightly larger than the rear one. The blisters indicated the position of the attachment points and could be seen slightly outboard and slightly to the rear of the twin Skybolt blisters under each wing.

On 8 May 1978 No. 27 Sqn received a further Vulcan B.Mk2 MRR. XH537 arrived complete with attachment points for the air-sampling pods bringing the squadron's total to nine aircraft. This aircraft was the original Skybolt test airframe in the early 1960s. XH537 eventually entered service with the RAF (31 May 1965) at Finningley with No. 230 OCU and continued serving with it for the next twelve years (OCU transferred to Scampton at the end of 1969). There have been reported sightings of this aircraft displaying No. 27 Sqn's Dumbo insignia and carrying the air- sampling pods in August 1977. Could it possibly have been 8 May 1977 and not May 1978 that the aircraft joined No. 27 Sqn?

When the Vulcans had their Terrain-Following Radar removed from the nose, a circular cap was placed over the hole. Three of the squadron's aircraft, XH534, XH537 and XH563, had never been modified during their service life to receive the radar. Upon close inspection of the aircraft's nose you can identify and place No. 27 Sqn's Vulcans in two groups — those with or without the cap. All nine of the Vulcans operated by the squadron also had two small white-blade aerials fitted to the top of the aircraft's nose. One other Vulcan (XL361) was also fitted with these aerials. Both Nos 35 and 617 Sqns had the MRR role assigned to them in an emergency in order to give assistance to No. 27 Sqn if required. It is interesting to note that XL361 had served with the squadron in the past and was responsible for conducting the first operational sortie (1 March 1974). From January 1975 to April 1981 XL361 remained at Scampton with Nos 35 and 617 Sqns, apart from two occasions when on loan to the A&AEE for a month at a time. XL361 appeared at RAF Finningley in July 1977 for the Royal Review (Jubilee Year) in the markings of No. 617 Sqn with the small white-blade aerials fitted.

In addition to the air-sampling pods, a smaller pod was positioned outboard of the port main undercarriage door. When removed, a small blister was placed over the attachment point. Only five of the squadron's B.Mk2 MRRs had all of the attachment points and blisters: XH534, XH537, XH558, XH560 and XH563 (all XH).

The nine Vulcans continued to serve with the squadron until 1981 when the Vulcan Force began to run down. It had been anticipated that

No. 27 Sqn with its specialized role would continue in service after the bomber squadrons had disbanded, but this would not be the case. The squadron's duties were to be passed onto the Nimrods at Kinloss and the air-sampling pods transferred to the VC10s at Brize Norton. The first of three Vulcans to leave the squadron in 1981 was XJ823, going to No. 35 Sqn on 2 April 1981. XJ823 originally entered service with No. 27 Sqn (21 April 1961) and was one of only five white Vulcans of the squadron displaying the elephant on the tail fin during their time in the nuclear free-fall bombing role 1961–62 (XH555, XH556, XJ823, XJ824 and XJ825). The oldest Vulcan in service (XH534) became the second to leave the squadron. XH534 was flown to St Athan (7 April 1981) to be placed in storage and then scrapped in 1982. On 16 April 1981 XJ825 followed in the footsteps of XJ823 and joined No. 35 Sqn.

No. 27 Sqn continued in service for a further eleven months until March 1982. On 23 March 1982 XH563 (the Sqn's first B.Mk2 MRR) was taken out of service and thankfully assigned for preservation at Scampton. The aircraft remained in position at Scampton displaying the following four Unit markings on its tail fin — Nos 27, 35 and 617 Sqns and No. 230 OCU — until November 1986. At that point apart from the aircraft's nose, the remainder of the airframe was scrapped. The day after XH563 came out of service, XH537 was flown to Abingdon (24 March

Figure 8.7:
Whilst on a routine patrol sortie on 16 October 1979, a No. 27 Sqn B.Mk2 MRR is seen by the workers at the Sullom Voe oil terminal in the north of Shetland. The workers welcomed these classic routine sights and sounds of the Vulcans but sadly there will be no more.
(Les Bulman)

1982) for preservation, but met the same fate as XH563 (scrapped, nose section currently preserved at Bruntingthorpe). On 25 March 1982 XH560 was transferred to Waddington and assigned to No. 44 Sqn. By 26 March 1982 only three Vulcans remained: XH558, XJ780 and XJ782. The squadron's final sortie was flown by XJ782 at the end of the month (31 March 1982). As No. 230 OCU, Nos 35 and 617 Sqns had disbanded, XJ782's last sortie for No. 27 Sqn had the significance of being the final Vulcan sortie from and to Scampton, although at a later date when Waddington's main runway was being resurfaced, No. 50 Sqn operated a number of its aircraft out of Scampton, e.g. XL426, XM652 and XM655. On the same day as XJ782's final sortie, XH558 with under-wing pods attached was allocated to No. 44 Sqn at Waddington. XJ780 had been declared Cat 5 for spares and then eventually scrapped on site at Scampton during 1982. Meanwhile XJ782 remained in service for a further six months at Waddington operating with No. 101 Sqn. These aircraft had been given a temporary reprieve due to the Falkland's crisis in the South Atlantic. XJ782 was flown for the very last time when it landed at RAF Finningley (Battle of Britain Air Show) on 4 September 1982 to be preserved at the station's main gate. In June 1988 the aircraft met its fate when it was sadly scrapped.

Three of No. 27 Sqn's Vulcans (XH558, XH560 and XJ825) remained in service with No. 50 Sqn at Waddington for a further two years until 31 March 1984 after conversion to K.Mk2 standard (air–air refuelling tankers).

No. 27 Sqn reformed in the early 1990s at RAF Marham equipped with Tornado GR.Mk1s.

After the disbandment of No. 27 Sqn on 31 March 1982, RAF Scampton's twenty-four-year relationship with the Avro Vulcan came to an end. All of the surviving aircraft were now stationed at RAF Waddington and it is to this station that we now return, back in 1968.

09

Continuing in Service in a New Era — Waddington

B Y MID-1968 the Waddington Wing had completely converted to the Vulcan B.Mk2. At that point in time the three squadrons, Nos 44, 50 and 101, were equipped with twenty-six Olympus 301 series Vulcans. This Bomber Wing was also operating three 201 series aircraft for varying lengths of time (XH558, XJ780 and XM571). This helped maintain the Wing's required strength (twenty-four), whilst some of the 301 series aircraft were out of service for modifications and servicing. The twenty-nine aircraft concerned were: XH557, XH558 (five-and-a-half-year attachment), XJ780, XM571, XM597–600, XM602, XM603, XM605–12, XM645 and XM648–57 (XM601 and XM604 w/o, XM646 and XM647 remained with the Cottesmore Wing).

All of the above Vulcans had by now received the Terrain-Following Radar (fitted to the aircraft's nose), having first been tested on XM606 during the second half of 1965 and throughout 1966. The next thing to

Figure 9.1:
RAF Waddington received its very first Vulcan B.Mk2, XH558, on 1 July 1960 and it was not until 23 March 1993 (thirty-three years) that the RAF's last remaining airworthy Vulcan B.Mk2, XH558, departed. **(Author's collection)**

note is the fitting of a further device, which began to appear on part of the Vulcan fleet during 1967. The item in question was the 'X band jammer'. This device helped to complement the Vulcan's existing ECM fit in an attempt to jam further Soviet threats such as airborne radars and therefore prevent detection. Only twenty-four Vulcan B.Mk2s of the Waddington Wing received this device. These were the surviving 301 series aircraft in mid-1968 from XM597–657, with the exception of XM645 (transferred to the OCU and missed out on the fitting of the 'X' band jammer), XM646 and XM647 (remained with the Cottesmore Wing). The aerial for the 'X band jammer' was fitted on the forward access door (ECM bay) under the aircraft's tail. At that point this unit only had a single-emitter head facing rearwards. In the early 1970s (c.1972) each aircraft (except XM610) had the unit replaced with an updated unit fitted with two aerials, covering front and rear. The original single-emitter had been tested on Vulcan B.Mk1A XA907 of the Bomber Command Development Unit at Finningley. The first B.Mk2 to conduct trials with the device was XH538 (1965–67) and two further B.Mk2s received the 'X band jammer' (single-emitter only) during the mid-1970s. The majority of the Waddington Wing Vulcans can be identified by the combination of 301 series engines, single ECM plate and the 'X band jammer' (1968–).

On 5 August 1968 XM645 (301 series engines) was flown to Finningley where it began operating with No. 230 OCU. In exchange for this aircraft, XH563 (201 series) of No. 230 OCU was allocated to the Waddington Wing the following day. XH563 remained with the Waddington Wing until 18 March 1969 when it then returned to the OCU. In the meantime XJ780 transferred to the Cottesmore Wing for four months before returning to Waddington (6 December 1968–18 March 1969). On 19 March 1969 (the day after XJ780 returned), XM571 was flown to Akrotiri in Cyprus where it become part of the NEAF Bomber Wing. In mid-1969 the two remaining 201 series Vulcans were taken out of service to receive manufacturer's modifications (XH558, 4 June–14 October 1969 and XJ780, 4 July–3 September 1969).

As the Royal Navy took over the nuclear responsibility on 30 June 1969, the Waddington Wing squadrons continued in service operating twenty-seven Vulcan B.Mk2s, retaining a tactical nuclear strike capability. It was on that very same day that XM649 arrived back at Waddington, having just received its manufacturer's modifications (28 May–30 June 1969). Just over five months later this aircraft was loaned to Min Tec (2 December 1969–21 January 1970). Twenty-nine days before the year ended XH558 was involved in a CAT 3R flying accident. After receiving the necessary repairs it was returned to flying duties with the Waddington Wing.

(See colour Plate 5)

During 1970 four further aircraft joined the Wing on a temporary basis: XH538 ex-S/W (29 April 1970–21 April 1971), XJ784 ex-NEAF (16 December 1970–18 August 1971), XL384 ex-S/W (5 June–27 November 1970) and XM575 ex-S/W (28 July–28 November 1970).

When Nos 9 and 35 Sqns moved to Cyprus in January 1969, their responsibilities for deployments to the Far East were handed over to the Waddington Wing (Nos 44, 50 and 101 Sqns). It was over a year later that No. 101 Sqn demonstrated its commitment by deploying eight Vulcans to Tengah in Singapore. The eight aircraft involved in the detachment and noted on the flight line at Tengah were: XM655, XM612, XM608, XM657, XM656, XM652, XM602 and XM609.

Early in 1971 the Waddington Wing lost one of its Vulcans when XM610 crashed at Wingate, Co. Durham after a fire had started in No. 1 engine spreading quickly to the No. 2 engine and then the port wing (8 January 1971). All five of the No. 44 Sqn crew eventually abandoned the crippled Vulcan safely as it became uncontrollable. Only fifteen days later on 23 February another of the Waddington Wing's Vulcan B.Mk2s had a near disaster with an engine fire that followed an explosion. XM608 had just reached 200 ft after take-off when an explosion occurred and a fire broke out in the wing beneath the engine. The Captain, Flt Lt M. Paley, and his crew carried out the necessary emergency drills whilst

Figure 9.2:
Eight Vulcan B.Mk2s of No. 101 Sqn seen on the flight line at Tengah, Singapore in January 1970 (it returned to the UK in February). The aircraft had flown westbound from the UK (via the USA) to reach its destination ('Sunflower' detachment). Notice that XM609 has yet to be repainted (numerous patches of faded paint) and has therefore not received the 'white square' background (for the first-aid cross) on the emergency equipment bay panel (see Chapter 10).
(CBV via Alan Chapman)

Figure 9.3:
On 28 January 1970, whilst on the previously mentioned 'Sunflower' detachment, XM602 is seen here showing the flag in Hong Kong (Kia-Tak). Notice that the Terrain-Following Radar has been removed from the tip of the aircraft's nose and replaced by a circular 'cap' (fairing).
(Crown Copyright)

in the circuit, even though parts of the burning wing were falling away. Although the Vulcan was over weight, the Captain carried out a perfect asymmetric landing and XM608 along with the crew had been saved. The Queens Commendation was quite rightly awarded to Paley.

Three months later on 21 April 1971 XM645 returned from the OCU to serve once again with the Waddington Wing. The aircraft was exchanged with XH538, which made the reverse journey to join the OCU on the same day.

Towards the end of the year XM597 was attached to the A&AEE at Boscombe Down for about fifteen months (29 November 1971–12 February 1973), although it did return to the Waddington Wing for just over three weeks in 1972 (11 September–4 October). This aircraft had gone away to be fitted with, and then test, a Radar Warning Receiver placed on the top of the tail fin. This equipment now gave the Vulcan's tail a rectangular appearance and was fitted to all the remaining Vulcans in service during 1975–77. Before XM597 departed Waddington on 29 November 1971, the Waddington Wing received a replacement in the form of XM574 of No. 27 Sqn (301 series engines), which was allocated to No. 101 Sqn on 3 November 1971. At the conclusion of the trials XM597 served for six months with the Waddington Wing before being allocated to No. 101 Sqn in August 1973, allowing XM574 to be flown to

Figure 9.4:
XM597 of No. 101 Sqn seen fitted with the passive ECM tail fin whilst on static display at Leuchars on 15 September 1973.
(John Huggon)

Cyprus and join the NEAF Bomber Wing (24 August 1973). Back in August 1972 a further ex-Scampton Wing Vulcan (XM594) transferred to the Waddington Wing having just received its manufacturer's modifications, which had commenced five months earlier on 29 March 1972 (disbandment of No. 27 Sqn). During 1972 the Waddington Wing aircraft began to be identified by the Lincoln coat of arms on their tail. Also during that time some of the aircraft began to receive the low-visibility red/blue national markings and matt camouflage.

In 1972, as a demonstration that the Vulcan Force was still a global force, No. 44 Sqn deployed four Vulcans and embarked on a round-the-world flight which began on 23 January and lasted for five weeks. At about that time XM609 had been noted displaying the Lincoln coat of arms and a squadron badge on its tail fin. The markings portrayed the side view of an elephant on a white circular background. Both Nos 27 and 44 Sqns' official badge depicts an elephant (Indian and African elephant respectively). No. 27 Sqn's Vulcans at that point displayed the larger Dumbo elephant on their tail fin, so presumably XM609 could well have

Figure 9.5:
Having participated in the aircraft scramble along with XM645 and XM603, XM655 is seen coming in to land at Finningley on 18 September 1971.
(John Huggon)

Craig Bulman

Figure 9.6:
Seen on Finningley's ORP on 18 September 1971 is XM645 of the Waddington Wing. After taking part in the aircraft scramble, XM645 went on to conduct a flying display at Biggin Hill. (**John Huggon**)

been one of the four aircraft involved in the previously mentioned detachment. It may well have been the case that this aircraft was portraying an early No. 44 Sqn insignia, but only for the five weeks of the detachment, before being returned to the Waddington Wing. Two further Vulcans of the Waddington Wing, XM607 and XM657, were also noted displaying what appeared to be a side view of an elephant painted white/grey on the tail fin. On that occasion the former aircraft also had the black panther's head of Strike Command on the forward fuselage and was noted at RNZAF Ohakea on a detachment with three other Vulcans from Waddington. The small white (elephant) symbol was placed directly below the Lincoln coat of arms in the case of XM607, whilst it appeared immediately to the right of the red/white/blue fin flash on XM657. These markings could possibly have been another early example of No. 44 Sqn's insignia whilst its aircraft were deployed to the Far East.

(See colour Plate 6)

Towards the end of 1972 the Vulcans allocated to the Waddington Wing were: XH557, XH558, XM574, XM594, XM598–600, XM602,

Figure 9.7:
XM655 of the Waddington Wing in 1970–71; notice the 'X band jammer' under the aircraft's tail section. (**APN**)

XM603, XM605–9, XM611, XM612, XM645 and XM648–57 (twenty-seven *(See colour Plate 7)* in total, providing it with three spare). Out of these Vulcans, XM574, XM649, XM607 and XM603 participated in the four aircraft scramble at the Finningley Air Show on 16 September 1972.

In May 1972 XH558 was allocated to No. 101 Sqn and remained with it until departing to Bitteswell on 17 August 1973 (conversion to B.Mk2 MRR). At the beginning of 1973 XL387 of No. 230 OCU, fitted with 301 series engines, joined the Waddington Wing (10 January). It was this aircraft that No. 101 Sqn had allocated to it during August 1973 after XH558 had departed.

During 1974 a number of changes took place, beginning with two of the original 301 series Vulcans (XH557 and XM645) that both lacked the 'X band jammer'. These two aircraft were flown to Cyprus to join the NEAF (19 April and 12 March respectively). The Waddington Wing received its first replacement in the form of XL388 ex-No. 617 Sqn on 1 April. This was followed by XM575 on 15 April 1974 transferring from the same squadron. A third Vulcan XL389 also from No. 617 Sqn joined the Waddington Wing on 26 June 1974. XL388 had been involved in a CAT 3R flying accident on 18 June 1974 but was soon repaired and returned to service. Earlier in the year RAF St Athan completed the one hundredth major service of a Vulcan B.Mk2. No. 101 Sqn's commanding officer, Wg Cdr Eric Macey, collected the aircraft (XM605) and returned it to RAF Waddington on 9 February 1974.

It was during 1974 that four of the Waddington Wing's Vulcans set off for Barksdale AFB, Louisiana, USA, to participate in the SAC Bombing competition 'Giant Voice' (10–16 November), competing against fifty-two American crews. All four Vulcans involved (XM599, XM606, XM649

Figure 9.8:
Now painted with the toned-down red/blue national markings and the matt camouflage scheme, XM603 is seen during a display at Woodford on 23 June 1973. Notice that the rear of the large radome has remained white (bib).
(John Huggon)

Craig Bulman

Figure 9.9:
*Having participated
in the 1974 Giant
Voice Bombing
and Navigation
Competition, XM653
is back at
Waddington display-
ing the Union Jack
on the tail fin and
No. 1 Group's pan-
ther head on the for-
ward fuselage. (APN)*

and XM653) displayed a Union Jack on the tail fin as well as the black panther's head of No. 1 Group on the side of the forward fuselage. XM599 and XM606 were at that point displaying their new matt camouflage and light grey underside but retained the white on the rear of the radome (bib). The other two aircraft retained their glossy coating over the camouflage but had received the low-visibility red/blue roundels. Some of the best results ever were achieved during the competition, including the winning of the Mathis Trophy (best crew in bombing and celestial navigation) for the first time by an RAF crew. This trophy had been awarded to Flt Lt Peter Perry and his crew from No. 230 OCU who showed that it really was possible to achieve first class results with the Vulcan Bombers, even though the American aircraft (B52s/F111s) had far more up-to-date equipment fitted. Flt Lt Patrick Langdown and his crew from No. 101 Sqn won the Navigation Trophy, whilst the best Vulcan sortie, including a direct hit on the target, was won by a No. 44 Sqn crew Captained by Flt Lt Rodger Morris.

Although there were numerous bombing and navigation competitions over the years there was a further trophy, known as the Medium Bomber Efficiency Trophy, for which to compete. This was presented to the most efficient medium bomber squadron. It was originally presented in 1955 by Mr A.G. Townley, Australian Minister for Air, on behalf of No. 460 Sqn (Royal Australian Air Force) in memory of one thousand of this squadron's aircrew killed in action during the Second World War. During the War No. 460 Sqn operated Avro Lancaster B.Is and B.IIIs from RAF Breighton in Yorkshire (September 1942–May 1943) before moving to RAF Binbrook in Lincolnshire (May 1943–July 1945). Although the

Lancasters have long since gone from these two decommissioned ex-Bomber Command Airfields, Breighton still echoes to the sound of Merlin engines to this day. It is here, on a small airstrip in the south-east corner of the original airfield, that preserved airworthy examples of Spitfire and Hurricane aircraft are lovingly maintained. By competing for the Medium Bomber Efficiency Trophy during the late 1950s-early 1980s, the V-Bomber squadrons played a part in remembering the aircrew of No. 460 Sqn (Royal Australian Air Force). Winning examples include No. 83 Sqn Vulcan B.Mk2 1961 and No. 101 Sqn Vulcan B.Mk1 1963.

At the end of 1974 the following twenty-eight Vulcans were allocated to the Waddington Wing: XL387–9, XM575, XM594, XM597–600, XM602, XM603, XM605–9, XM611, XM612 and XM648–57. At that point five of the Vulcans were away at the manufacture's facilities receiving modifications (XM599 3 December 1974–8 August 1975, XM603 9 August 1974–5 June 1975, XM607 14 June 1974–25 March 1975, XM609 28 March 1974–5 February 1975 and XM656 21 October 1974–2 July 1975). This would have left twenty-three aircraft remaining for the three squadrons. XM651 now had the grey camouflage (matt finish) extended over the black radome and was on display to the public at the Finningley Air Show, positioned on the Operational Readiness Platform. Alongside this aircraft

Figure 9.10: *Posing for a squadron photo in 1974 are members of No. 44 (Rhodesia) Sqn at Waddington. Although the Vulcan in the background has yet to be positively identified, it is understood to be one of the following seven aircraft: XM575, XM594*, XM598, XM648*, XM651*, XM654* or XM656 (*had been flown by No. 44 Sqn crews at about that time).*
(CBV via John Hathaway)

was XM652 that still displayed the original red/white/blue roundels, glossy finish, white underside and black radome.

Early in the new year the three resident squadrons at Waddington were to be joined by No. 9 Sqn, returning to the UK after serving six years at Akrotiri in Cyprus.

In January 1975 the Vulcans of No. 9 Sqn arrived at Waddington in two waves. The first of these arrived on 15 January 1975 consisting of XH557, XJ784, XM645 and XM647. These aircraft were followed two days later on the 17th by XJ780, XJ823, XL391 and XM646. With the exception of XM574 of No. 35 Sqn that went to Scampton, all of the 301 series Vulcans of the NEAF were allocated to No. 9 Sqn (XH557, XJ784, XL391, XM645, XM646 and XM647).

It was during 1975 that each squadron reapplied its individual Unit markings to the Vulcans. No. 9 Sqn painted its insignia, depicting a green bat, on a yellow circular background. All of the Waddington aircraft

Figure 9.11: *Three members of a No. 44 Sqn crew (John Hathaway, AEO, Jimmy Robb, Nav Radar, and Ash Weaver, Nav Plotter, Captained by Sqn Ldr Dave Haller) seen on a routine high-level bombing and navigation sortie at some point over the North Sea. The detail on the map shows an 'IP' (initial point) on the north Lincolnshire coast, then northbound to Orkney, then heading south passing over Lossiemouth and Leuchars to about East Midlands Airport. The flight then heads northbound again passing what looks like Leeming and Newcastle Airport to about Holy Island and presumably returning to Waddington. (CBV via John Hathaway)*

continued to display the Lincoln coat of arms on their tail fin.

On 9 July 1975 XJ780 arrived at Bitteswell to receive manufacturer's modifications. On completion of this work it returned to No. 9 Sqn at Waddington (31 March 1976). During July and August 1975 the squadron's total dropped back to seven aircraft, although two Vulcans of No. 230 OCU were loaned to the Waddington Wing to help maintain numbers throughout the summer/autumn of 1975 (XL318 18 June–5 August, XL360 8 August–21 October). No. 9 Sqn received two additional aircraft of its own during September when XM609 of the Waddington Wing and XM653 of No. 44 Sqn both had the 'green bat' insignia applied to them.

During October 1975 Flt Lt Alcock and his crew of No. 9 Sqn were on detachment to Malta flying XM645, fitted with the new rectangular RWR at the top of its tail fin but still displaying a black radome. As the Vulcan approached RAF Luqa on the 14th the aircraft unfortunately undershot the runway and the port main undercarriage was pushed up into the wing. Flt Lt Alcock regained control as the aircraft bounced back into the air, then climbed the Vulcan away in an attempt to gain enough height for the 'five' rear crew to bail out. After initial impact with the ground a fire started that led to an explosion during the climb and the aircraft began to break up. The Captain and Co-Pilot ejected safely but the rest of the crew was all killed in the crash. The remains of the Vulcan fell onto the village of Zabbar. Coincidentally, Flt Lt Alcock had been the Captain of XM610 that crashed at Wingate, Co. Durham in 1971 after an engine fire.

On 5 December 1975 XM602 of the Waddington Wing joined No. 9 Sqn (returning from manufacturer's modifications, which commenced on 26 March 1975), bringing the total allocation to nine (XH557, XJ784, XJ823, XL391, XM602, XM609, XM646, XM647 and XM653).

On the nights of 5–12 April 1976 the annual bombing and navigation competition (Double Top) took place over the UK against USAF B52Gs. All six Vulcan Bomber squadrons participated. Selected crews of the three Victor tanker squadrons (Nos 55, 57 and 214), along with No. 27 Sqn operating its Vulcan B.Mk2 MRRs, competed in the navigation phase only. A crew from No. 9 Sqn won the 'Laurence Minot' Trophy for the best overall RAF crew. The same squadron then won the 'Armaments Officers' Trophy for the best RAF squadron and also the 'Sasson' Trophy for the best RAF squadron at navigation. With a total of 1329 points, Flt Lt Deveson and his crew of No. 9 Sqn became runners-up in the overall competition, after being beaten by only eleven points by a B52G of the 320th Bomber Wing. Flt Lt Phurston and his crew of No. 44 Sqn won the 'Electronics' Trophy for the best individual crew in navigation.

Figure 9.12:
Whilst on a low-level exercise over Colorado, XM653 of No. 9 Sqn collided with an American Bald Eagle (bird strike). The aircraft is seen after the Captain, Sqn Ldr Peter Mayes and his crew, which included Flt Lt John Hathaway No. 44 Sqn (AEO), returned to Offut AFB, where the extent of the damage is being assessed. After considerable maintenance in the UK (Waddington), XM653 was air tested on 12 May 1976 (seven months later) by a No. 44 Sqn crew. The prolonged absence of this aircraft probably explains why XM602 of the Waddington Wing was issued to No. 9 Sqn after the completion of its manufacturer's modifications (5 December 1975).
(CBV via John Hatherway)

Figure 9.13 (inset):
Close up of the damage caused to XM653 on 31 October 1975. **(CBV via John Hathaway)**

During 1976 there were a number of differences between the individual Vulcans on the squadron. XM602 now had the passive ECM fin tip antenna (RWR), as did XM646, although the latter aircraft still had its black radome. XJ784 also retained the black radome but with the underside of the aircraft remaining white (not yet fitted with passive ECM). Other Vulcans on the squadron displayed the up-to-date matt camouflage but had yet to be fitted with the passive ECM fin tip antenna.

In April 1976 XJ780 had returned to the squadron whilst XM609 transferred to No. 44 Sqn and was substituted by XM649 of No. 101 Sqn. Two months later XL389 of the Waddington Wing was allocated to No. 9 Sqn (June). On 23 November 1976 XJ780 was then allocated to No. 27 Sqn at Scampton and in return for this aircraft No. 27 Sqn transferred XM569 to No. 9 Sqn two days later (displaying the 'bat' insignia by the new year). The squadron's current allocation of aircraft remained high until the summer of 1978. During October 1976 XM602 is shown to have been operating with No. 230 OCU and No. 35 Sqn (19–29 October and 29 October–1 November 1976, respectively).

In the new year, XJ823 departed to St Athan for servicing and modification to the MRR role pending its transfer to No. 27 Sqn (27 April 1977). Coming in the opposite direction in exchange was XL427 (ex-No. 27 Sqn) on 2 May 1977. On 21 June 1977 XM653 headed for Bitteswell to receive manufacturer's modifications. The following month two aircraft of No. 9 Sqn appeared at RAF Finningley for the Queens Jubilee celebrations.

Figure 9.14:
After taking part in the four aircraft scramble XM605 No. 101 Sqn, XL427 No. 9 Sqn and XM654 No. 50 Sqn conduct a fly-past at Waddington on 17 June 1978 (XM573 No. 44 Sqn gave the solo display).
(Author's collection)

Figure 9.15:
Cpl Triner, RAF, with three young invited guests at the closing down ceremony of RAF Luqa, Malta. The Vulcan Bomber that attended the ceremony was XM569 of No. 9 Sqn on 13 September 1978.

(Richard Triner)

XL389 was positioned on the operational readiness platforms poised ready for a scramble demonstration, whilst XM646 was in the static display. By the end of 1977 the ten aircraft known to be operating with and displaying the markings of No. 9 Sqn were: XH557, XJ784, XL389, XL391, XL427, XM569, XM602, XM646, XM647 and XM649.

On 27 January 1978 XM653 returned from Bitteswell and by June 1978 this aircraft was operating with and displaying the markings of No. 101 Sqn. Two more of No. 9 Sqn's Vulcans took their turn at Bitteswell for modifications during 1978: XM647 (21 July 1978–31 May 1979) and XL391 (2 November 1978–31 July 1979). In December 1978 No. 9 Sqn had on strength XH557, XJ784, XL389, XL427, XM569, XM602, XM646 and XM649.

Throughout 1979 six of No. 9 Sqn's Vulcans were to be exchanged with the other three Waddington squadrons. A further aircraft, XH557, would also be leaving the squadron but only to receive manufacturer's modifications at Bitteswell (20 March 1979–1 February 1980). In May XM597 arrived from No. 50 Sqn, XM607 came from No. 44 Sqn and XM647 returned from Bitteswell. In exchange No. 50 Sqn took over XM569 and No. 44 Sqn received XJ784 (both aircraft were displaying the appropriate squadron's insignia by June). The next movement occurred in June when XM606 was transferred from No. 101 Sqn. In the same month XM602 was seen with No. 50 Sqn's insignia on its tail (No. 9 Sqn until at least 10 April). During July there were further movements when XL391 returned from Bitteswell to rejoin the squadron and XL389 was then

(See colour Plate 8) transferred to No. 44 Sqn. In August XM649 joined No. 101 Sqn and in

September XM647 transferred to No. 44 Sqn, whilst XM651 moved from No. 50 Sqn to join No. 9 Sqn. The squadron received one more Vulcan during October when XM598 transferred from No. 50 Sqn. Confused? By the end of 1979 No. 9 Sqn had eight Vulcan B.Mk2s allocated to it: XL391, XL427, XM597, XM598, XM606, XM607, XM646 and XM651.

Only one of the squadron's aircraft made the trip to Bitteswell for manufacturer's modifications during 1980 (XM607, 25 March–18 December 1980). By June 1980 XL391 had transferred to No. 101 Sqn and could be seen by the public at the annual Open Day inside one of Waddington's hangars displaying the new insignia. In September No. 9 Sqn took delivery of XM648 from No. 101 Sqn. This was one of the thirteen Vulcans that received the wrap-round camouflage during their final years of squadron service. Three months later No. 101 Sqn handed over another of its aircraft (XM656) to No. 9 Sqn (December 1980). By that point the squadron had an allocation of ten aircraft: XH557, XL427, XM597, XM598, XM606, XM607, XM646, XM648, XM651 and XM656.

With plans for the Vulcan Force to start running down during 1981 there would be further changes to the squadron's current allocation of aircraft. 'The pack was about to be reshuffled.' In March 1981 XH557 transferred to No. 50 Sqn and XM607 moved over to No. 101 Sqn. On 6 April 1981 XM608 of No. 50 Sqn became one of the earlier Vulcans to be taken out of service and declared CAT 5C at St Athan. A replacement was received during April 1981 when XL427 of No. 9 Sqn (now with wrap-round camouflage) transferred to No. 50 Sqn. In October 1981 No. 50 Sqn received XM598 from No. 9 Sqn and at that point XL427 was returned to display the bat insignia once again.

Going back to April 1981, No. 9 Sqn's allocation had been reduced by three (XH557, XL427 and XM607), but the squadron received three other Vulcans during the same month. XL361 (ex-No. 35 Sqn) arrived from Scampton displaying its previous Unit's insignia, which it retained for at least two further months. The squadron then received XL444 (ex-No. 35 Sqn) with its wrap-round camouflage, followed by XM573 (shown as transferring from No. 230 OCU). At the annual Waddington Open Day during the following month (May 1981), nine of the squadron's ten aircraft were on view to the public: XL361 (No. 35 Sqn's insignia), XL444 (static display), XM598 and XM656 (in the hangars), XM648 (ORP-scramble), XM573, XM597, XM606 and XM646 (all parked out on the airfield's dispersals). Only XM651 was absent.

Transferring from No. 35 Sqn in June 1981 was XH562. The aircraft had been with No. 9 Sqn in the past as part of the NEAF in Cyprus. XH562 was also the No. 9 Sqn aircraft that had the roundels on its nose

Figure 9.16:
A truly 'classic' sight that most people could only dream of was the sight and sound of a Vulcan Bomber at low-level going about its routine training. XM597 of No. 9 Sqn is seen here during a low-level run at Spadeadam on 15 April 1981. Notice the aircraft's shadow in the first picture (the sheep must have had a good view).
(John Huggon)

'Zapped' whilst in New Zealand in 1972 (Kiwi painted in the centre of the roundel). When No. 9 Sqn took delivery of this aircraft in June 1981 it transferred XM646 to No. 101 Sqn. XM646 had served with No. 9 Sqn for the longest period of time since its return to the UK in 1975 (six-and-a-half years).

Although there was less than a year remaining before the squadron disbanded, further exchanges took place. During September 1981 XM572 of No. 35 Sqn transferred to Waddington to join No. 9 Sqn and in the same month XM648 was returned to No. 101 Sqn. As previously mentioned, in October XM598 swapped places with XL427 of No. 50 Sqn and XM597 joined No. 101 Sqn.

During November 1981 XL361 was at Goose Bay, Canada. This station became a frequent training location throughout the existence of the V-Force for visiting Vulcan crews to conduct and practice low-level flying sorties. Whilst at Goose Bay on 13 November ('Friday 13th'), XL361 sustained CAT 3 damage. The aircraft was unable to return home at that point and had to remain at the base until a team of inspectors was flown out from the UK. On 21 December 1981 the inspectors deemed XL361 'not worth repairing' taking into account the fact that the Vulcan Force had already began to run down. The aircraft was therefore declared CAT 5 and written off. Although XL361 had been abandoned at Goose Bay due to being unserviceable, work began on the airframe as it had been agreed that the Vulcan was to be preserved at the base. XL361 remains on display as a reminder and symbol of the past.

At the beginning of 1982 the following eight Vulcans remained with No. 9 Sqn: XH562, XL427, XL444, XM572, XM573, XM606, XM651 and XM656. The squadron had been earmarked to disband at Waddington on 29 April 1982 but until then they continued to operate the same eight aircraft. By the end of March 1982 all four Units at Scampton had disbanded. The remaining Vulcans were now all stationed at RAF Waddington equipping four squadrons. On 1 April 1982 there were thirty-seven Vulcans remaining in service: XH557, XH558, XH560–2, XJ782, XJ784, XJ823, XJ825, XL319, XL321, XL360, XL386, XL388, XL391, XL426, XL427, XL444, XL445, XM569, XM571–3, XM575, XM594, XM597, XM598, XM606, XM607, XM612, XM647, XM648, XM651, XM652 and XM654–6. Suddenly, taking everyone by surprise, the Argentine forces invaded the Falkland Islands.

Although the Avro Vulcan was in its eleventh hour some of the aircraft were prepared for action during the coming days and weeks after orders had been given on 9 April for possible involvement if diplomatic talks failed. As originally planned No. 9 Sqn disbanded at the end of April 1982. The aircraft were retained and distributed between the remaining squadrons, although two of its aircraft were flown to the USA to be preserved. The first was XM573 going to Offut AFB (22 May), followed by XM606 to Barksdale AFB on 7 June. After the squadron's disbandment, XH562 joined No. 101 Sqn and XL427 transferred to No. 44 Sqn. XM656 that was flown to RAF Cottesmore on 9 August for display (eventually scrapped, with the exception of the aircraft's nose) and the remaining three Vulcans, XL444, XM572 and XM651, were declared CAT 5C on 10 September and then scrapped on site in the December.

No. 9 Sqn reformed at RAF Honnington in June 1982 as the first squadron to operate the Tornado GR.Mk1.

Out of all the Vulcan squadrons No. 101 at Waddington operated the

Vulcan Bombers longer than any of the others (nearly twenty-five years, October 1957–August 1982). When the squadron was stationed at Finningley during the late 1950s its Vulcan B.Mk1s wore the Unit's crest on their tail fin. With the introduction of centralized servicing in the early 1960s, after the squadron had moved to Waddington, these markings were removed. It was not until 1975 that No. 101 Sqn began to reapply the Unit's insignia onto its aircraft.

During 1975 aircraft of the Waddington Wing were slowly but surely being attached to an individual squadron and the appropriate Unit's insignia applied onto the tail fin whilst retaining the Lincoln coat of arms. One of the earliest aircraft, if not the first, to display No. 101 Sqn's insignia placed inside a sloping number '101' was XM575. At that point (May 1975) XM575 still had its black radome, white underside and red/white/blue roundels but had yet to be fitted with rectangular fairing at the top of its tail fin. During May 1975 XM648, which had operated with the squadron since August 1973, transferred to No. 44 Sqn and in its place No. 101 Sqn received XM612 (ex-WW). This was followed in June by the allocation of XM594 (ex-WW) to No. 101 Sqn. By September 1975 the following eight aircraft had been allocated to the squadron: XM575, XM594, XM600, XM605, XM611, XM612, XM655 and XM656. During 1975/76 eight other Vulcan B.Mk2s are also thought to have operated with No. 101 Sqn, but it is unknown whether they actually had the appropriate markings applied. Both XM597 and XM598 transferred to No. 44 Sqn (September and August 1975 respectively). XM649 transferred to No. 9 Sqn (April 1976), whilst XL387, XM599 and XM657 joined No. 50 Sqn in August 1975. This squadron also received XM654 in September 1975 and XM651 in May 1976. The latter aircraft left No. 101 Sqn on 7 August 1975 initially to go to Bitteswell for manufacturer's modifications before joining No. 50 Sqn on 21 May 1976.

After being allocated a further aircraft during December 1975 (XM606 ex-WW), No. 101 Sqn flew XM605 to Bitteswell to receive manufacturer's modifications (23 December 1975–30 September 1976). On 9 July 1976 XM594 took some time out when it also went to Bitteswell for modifications (returned 31 March 1977). Pending the return of XM605 at the end of September, the squadron sent XM611 to Bitteswell to begin its modification work, which took nine months to complete (28 September 1976–24 June 1977). XM605 eventually returned to No. 101 Sqn on 6 October 1976. By the end of 1976 the number of aircraft on the squadron had been reduced to seven (XM575, XM600, XM605, XM606, XM612, XM655 and XM656), but it would unexpectedly drop back further in January.

(See colour Plate 9)

On 17 January 1977 XM600 was flying over the Lincolnshire country-side when a fire broke out in the bomb bay. The crew took the necessary actions in an attempt to extinguish the fire but to no avail as it had quickly spread to the port wing. After orders from the Captain the crew abandoned the aircraft, although one member was injured. XM600 crashed near Spilsby, about twenty-six miles east of Waddington. Five days after the loss of XM600, another Vulcan of No. 101 Sqn was flown to Bitteswell to receive manufacturer's modifications. The aircraft concerned was XM612, which would be away from the squadron for the next nine months (24 January–10 October 1977). By February the number of aircraft attached to the squadron was five. Pending the return of XM594 at the end of March, No. 101 Sqn was allocated two further Vulcans in order to return the squadron to full strength. By March both XM648 (ex-No. 44 Sqn) and XM657 (ex-No. 50 Sqn) were displaying the markings of No. 101 Sqn. At the end of March 1977 the squadron's allocation consisted of XM575, XM594, XM605, XM606, XM648 and XM655–7. This total was temporarily reduced when XM594 transferred to No. 44 Sqn during May 1977, where the Unit's insignia was applied to the tail fin. No. 101 squadron's total returned to normal when XM611 arrived back from Bitteswell on 24 June. Early in October 1977 XM606 was flown to Bitteswell in preparation for its manufacturer's modifications (6 October 1977–27 July 1978), with the knowledge that the work on XM612 would be completed a few days later (10th). The squadron continued to operate its current eight aircraft for the next eight months (XM575, XM605, XM611, XM612, XM648 and XM655–7) until the next aircraft had to go to Bitteswell. XM655 began its nine-month stay (23 June 1978–26 March 1979) at the manufacture's facilities were it received further modifications. Also in June 1978 XM575 was transferred to No. 50 Sqn, and No. 101 Sqn received XM653 from No. 9 Sqn. Returning to the squadron on 27 July was XM606, bringing the total back to eight aircraft (XM605, XM606, XM611, XM612, XM648, XM653, XM656 and XM657). In October 1978 all of No. 101 Sqn's personnel, commanded by Wg Cdr Mike Harrington, lined up in front of XM657 for a photo session to celebrate twenty-one years of flying Vulcans. This was longer than any of the other Vulcan squadrons. During December 1978 a detachment of four Vulcans from Scampton and Waddington flew to Nellis AFB to participate in exercise Red Flag alongside the Americans. Crews from all six Vulcan Bomber squadrons took part in the event. XM612 at that point in time displayed No. 50 Sqn's insignia (at least on the port side of its tail fin) and XM657 was indicated as being with No. 44 Sqn. Both XM612 and XM657 were seen with No. 101 Sqn's insignia in the months running up to and after the event.

Figure 9.17:
*Climbing away from
Waddington's run-
way 03 is XM605 of
No. 101 Sqn on 17
June 1978.*
(John Huggon)

Figure 9.18:
*XM657 of No. 101
Sqn is seen over
shooting after a prac-
tice approach at
Carlisle Airport on
26 October 1978.
Notice the landing
lights under the air-
craft's wing.*
(John Huggon)

During May and June 1979 further changes were made. In May XM605 transferred to No. 50 Sqn and XM653 returned to No. 9 Sqn, then in June No. 9 Sqn received XM606. It was at that point that XM655 received a major service and a fresh coat of paint whilst at St Athan. By July 1979 XM653 had moved back to No. 101 Sqn. At the beginning of August 1979 the aircraft attached to the squadron were: XM611, XM612, XM648, XM653 and XM655–7.

On 9 August 1979 XM653 became unserviceable and was declared CAT 3, which required the attention of a maintenance unit. Just over a month later XM653 was flown to St Athan to receive further attention (10 September). The aircraft was then placed in storage until 19 September 1980 when it was re-declared CAT 5C (salvage of useful components). By the end of December 1980 the aircraft had been placed onto the station's dump and was later scrapped (August 1981). XM653 had become the first casualty in the run-down of the Vulcan Force after flying 4,391.30 hrs.

The squadron's numbers had now dropped, but help was at hand because XM649 of No. 9 Sqn transferred across to take over from XM653 in August 1979. Three further aircraft from Scampton were attached to the Waddington Wing during that time, helping to maintain numbers throughout the four squadrons: XM571 of No. 617 Sqn (8 August– 4 December 1979), XL318 of No. 230 OCU (7 November 1979–21 February 1980) and XH538 that had been at Waddington since 16 August 1978 and remained until 23 November 1979, when it then returned to No. 35 Sqn.

On 1 February 1980 XM656 began its nine-month stay at Bitteswell, returning to No. 101 Sqn on 13 October 1980. Over the coming months there were a number of changes. The youngest Vulcan in service, XM657, which by now had been repainted in the wrap-round camouflage, joined No. 44 Sqn in April 1980. The next to move was XM602 of No. 50 Sqn, which had transferred to No. 101 Sqn and was displaying its insignia by May 1980. In June XM652 (the first Vulcan to have the wrap-round camouflage) was displaying a smaller version of No. 101 Sqn's insignia, painted over the top of the white circular disc of its previous Unit (No. 44 Sqn). This appears to have been a temporary move as it was soon back with No. 44 Sqn's markings on its tail. Also in June three other Olympus 301 series aircraft joined the squadron: XL391, XJ784 and XL389 (Nos 9, 44 and 44 Sqn respectively). The latter aircraft was now displaying the new wrap-round camouflage scheme. At about this time XM648 had been flown to St Athan for a major service, so by the end of June 1980 the squadron's allocation consisted of XJ784, XL389, XL391, XM602, XM611, XM612, XM649, XM652 and XM655. Over the next few months two more of the squadron's aircraft left for manufacturer's modifications: XM602 (4 July 1980–31 March 1981) and XM612 (15 August 1980–7 May 1981). No. 101 Sqn lost another of its Vulcans in September when XM648 joined No. 9 Sqn after returning from St Athan with the wrap-round camouflage but No. 101 Sqn received XM603 ex-No. 50 Sqn as a replacement. XM656, having returned to the squadron in October from Bitteswell, was trans- ferred to No. 9 Sqn in December. At the end of 1980 the squadron was operating the following seven aircraft: XJ784, XL389, XL391, XM603, XM611, XM649 and XM655 (XM652 had by then returned to No. 44 Sqn).

During March 1981 the squadron's total increased to nine when XM607 transferred from No. 9 Sqn and XM602 returned from Bitteswell on the 31st. Six days later the first Vulcan to be withdrawn from service displaying the wrap-round camouflage arrived at St Athan. XL389 was withdrawn from active duty and was declared CAT 5C after flying 5,741.05 hrs. On 12 May 1981 XM612 returned from Bitteswell and during the same month No. 44 Sqn handed over XL386 to No. 101 Sqn. A further aircraft was added to the squadron in June when XM646 transferred from No. 9 Sqn. By the end of June 1981 there were eleven Vulcans attached to No. 101 Sqn: XJ784, XL386, XL391, XM602, XM603, XM607, XM611, XM612, XM646, XM649 and XM655. This high allocation did not last for long. In July the squadron transferred XM603, XM607, XM612 and XM655 to No. 44 Sqn and in return received XJ824. During the same month celebrations took place at RAF Scampton to mark the twenty-fifth anniversary of the Vulcan. Each of the squadrons currently operating Vulcans had one aircraft on static display with the appropriate insignia on the tail fin. All of the remaining Units selected an aircraft with wrap-round camouflage with the exception of Nos 27 (MRR) and 101 Sqns which did not have one. No. 44 Sqn, however, had three of them (XM575, XM652 and XM657) and coincidentally, when the event took place on the 25th the representative aircraft for No. 101 Sqn was XM657. On 2 September 1981 XM649 was flown to St Athan where it was declared CAT 5C and its frontline service with the RAF ended with 5,384.25 hrs on the clock. As a replacement, XM648 was returned from No. 9 Sqn during the same month. The following month No. 9 Sqn also transferred XM597 to No. 101 Sqn. Throughout September and October XM654 of No. 50 Sqn is also shown to have operated with No. 101 Sqn, although it is understood to have retained No. 50 Sqn's insignia.

In the new year three Vulcans left the squadron and two arrived, returning the total to eight. The three aircraft that left the Unit were all flown to St Athan and stood down from active duty (XM602 and XM611 arrived on 7 January 1982 with XM646 following on the 26th). XM611 had operated with No. 101 Sqn since 1972. XM602 was initially preserved at the station's museum (Historic Aircraft Museum) until October 1992 when it was dismantled for transportation to a new location. However, the aircraft was eventually scrapped in 1993 with the exception of the aircraft's nose, which was sent to the Avro Aircraft Restoration Trust at Woodford (November 1993). At the beginning of January XM597 participated in 'Red Flag' at Nellis AFB. With the disbandment of No. 617 Sqn at the end of December 1981, XM571 transferred from that Unit to No. 101 Sqn on 8 January 1982. In the meantime No. 35 Sqn took over some of No. 617 Sqn's aircraft and boosted its numbers further. This allowed XL360, which still had plenty of hours left, to be allocated to No. 101 Sqn on 5 January 1982. As previously mentioned, XL360 appears to have remained at Scampton until at least 20 March 1982, but it had arrived at its new station by the 31st. Also during the March XJ824 made its last flight, which was to the Imperial War Museum at Duxford (13 March), to be preserved after flying 6,291.30 hrs. No. 101 Sqn received a replacement in the form of XJ825 during March. This aircraft was allocated to the squadron due to the fact that its previous Unit, No. 35 Sqn, had disbanded at the end of February. By the beginning of April 1982 No. 101 Sqn was operating XJ784, XJ825, XL360, XL386, XL391, XM571, XM597 and XM648. At that point (1 April), XL391 was in Canada whilst the remainder were all at their home base of Waddington.

With the Vulcan Force being run down, no one could have imagined that over the coming months four of No. 101 Sqn's aircraft were to receive a great deal of attention and modification as opposed to being scrapped. This was as a direct result of Argentine forces invading the Falkland Islands. Initially both XL391 and XM597 were prepared for possible bombing raids on the islands, whilst XJ825 and XM571 were converted into single-point tankers. The Vulcan tanker conversions were to provide a stopgap force in the UK as the bulk of the Victor K.Mk2s were deployed in the South Atlantic.

On 11 May both XJ825 and XM571 were flown to Woodford to begin their conversion into tankers and were designated K.Mk2. In May, as a replacement for these two aircraft, No. 101 Sqn received XH562 from the

Figure 9.19:
Arriving back at Waddington in early 1982 is XM597 of No. 101 Sqn. The aircraft is seen before deploying to Ascension in May 1982, before having the underside of the airframe painted dark sea grey and the squadron markings, together with the Lincoln coat of arms, removed from the tail fin.
(CBV via Craig Jackson)

Figure 9.20:
This shot of XM648 of No. 101 Sqn was taken between April 1982 (Falkland's War) and August 1982 (No. 101 Sqn disbanded). This can be determined by the lack of a flight-refuelling probe on this aircraft. From April 1982 most of the surviving Vulcans had the probes removed, to be used by the C130 Hercules and Nimrods involved in the Falkland's Campaign. During 1982 XM648 is known to have given a flying display at Cosford/Staverton on 5 May and Halton/ Brize Norton on 12 June. (CBV)

recently disbanded No. 9 Sqn and XJ782, previously of No. 27 Sqn. Both aircraft were displaying No. 101 Sqn's insignia by the end of June.

On 9 June 1982 XL360, along with five other Vulcans from Waddington, participated in a final farewell fly-over of Offutt AFB, Nebraska and marked the end of an era.

With only a matter of weeks remaining before No. 101 Sqn was due to disband (4 August 1982), plans were made for the relocation or disposal of its current aircraft. The two Vulcans involved in 'Operation Corporate' (Falkland's Campaign), XL391 and XM597 both had the Lincoln coat of arms and the Unit's insignia removed before having their undersides repainted in dark sea grey. Both aircraft had transferred to No. 44 Sqn and had the appropriate insignia applied to them after the Falkland's Campaign. At the time of disbandment in the August, No. 101 Sqn had six aircraft attached to it: XH562, XJ782, XJ784, XL360, XL386 and XM648. On 19 August XH562 made its final flight to RAF Catterick were it was used on the station's fire dump, after clocking up 5,978.20 hrs. During the same month XL360 transferred to No. 44 Sqn. The next disposal occurred on 26 August 1982, when XL386 was flown to RAF Manston and allocated to the Central Training Establishment where it survived until August 1993 before being scrapped. On 4 September 1982 XJ782 arrived at Finningley during the Annual Air Show where it was preserved and later became the station's gate guard. Like so many others,

however, this aircraft was later scrapped (June 1988). The remaining two Vulcans, XJ784 and XM648, were both declared CAT 5C (salvage of useful components) on 10 September 1982 and were later scrapped at Waddington (December 1982).

No. 101 Sqn reformed at RAF Brize Norton as a tanker squadron operating VC10 K.Mk2s on 1 May 1984 (at a later date, K.Mk3s and K.Mk4s).

The last Vulcan Unit to operate this aircraft in the bombing role was No. 44 'Rhodesia' Sqn. It came into existence as a Unit in August 1960 when No. 83 Sqn, with its B.Mk1s, was renumbered as No. 44 Sqn (No. 83 Sqn reformed at Scampton with the B.Mk2). During 1967 No. 44 Sqn began to exchange its aircraft for the B.Mk2s. Throughout the 1960s and early 1970s, due to centralized servicing, no Unit markings were applied to the aircraft. Occasionally, however, the Waddington station badge along with the Wing's three squadron badges (Nos 44, 50 and 101 Sqns) appeared on the crew entrance door. As previously mentioned XM609 had been noted with what appeared to be an early No. 44 Sqn badge in January 1972 (elephant on a white circular disc, similar to that of No. 27 Sqn). It was not until 1975 that No. 44 Sqn introduced onto its own aircraft, a numeral '44' badge on a white circular background outlined in black.

By May 1975 No. 44 Sqn was operating XH562, XJ782, XL388, XM648, XM650 and XM653 along with other shared Waddington Wing aircraft. Both XH562 and XJ782 were ex-NEAF Vulcans and the former aircraft had just returned from Bitteswell (9 May 1975), having received its manufacturer's modifications. In August the squadron's allocation further increased when XM598 received the squadron's insignia. In the same month XM648 was selected to receive modified burners to its 301 series Olympus engines (eight per engine) to conduct smoke suppression trials. Although a reduction in engine smoke emission was achieved, the exercise was deemed far too costly to equip the remaining thirty-seven 301 series Vulcans, possibly due to the aircraft's short planned life. During September 1975, XM653 transferred to No. 9 Sqn and the vacant slot in No. 44 Sqn was filled by XM652 of the Waddington Wing. Also in September XM598 was flown to Bitteswell to receive manufacturer's modifications (26 September 1975–9 July 1976). As a replacement for XM598, No. 44 Sqn received XM597 from No. 101 Sqn during the same month. Early in the new year two more of the squadron's aircraft were sent to Bitteswell for manufacturer's modifications (XM650 27 January–16 November 1976 and XM648 22 March 1976–11 January 1977). By March 1976 No. 44 Sqn's insignia had been applied to XM607 of the Waddington Wing. During the following month (April 1976) the

Figure 9.21:
XM650 of No. 44
Sqn at Leuchars on
9 September 1975.
(John Huggon)

squadron saw the departure of XM597, which transferred to No. 50 Sqn, followed by the arrival of XM609 from No. 9 Sqn. To help return the squadron's allocation to eight aircraft, No. 230 OCU handed over XL321 to No. 44 Sqn for a four months (8 June–8 November 1976). With the return of XM598 from Bitteswell in July 1976 the squadron consisted of XH562, XJ782, XL321, XL388, XM598, XM607, XM609 and XM652.

On 16 November 1976, XM650 returned to service with No. 44 Sqn and three days later (the 19th) XL388 made the reverse journey to Bitteswell. When XM648 returned on 11 January 1977, XM650 was then transferred to No. 50 Sqn. On 15 February 1977 XJ782 moved to the north of Lincoln to join No. 27 Sqn at Scampton and in return No. 44 Sqn received XM573 on 9 March. The squadron's allocation of aircraft dropped back to six (XH562, XM573, XM598, XM607, XM609 and XM652) when XM648 transferred to No. 101 Sqn in March, but increased slightly when XM594 of No. 101 Sqn joined No. 44 Sqn in May 1977. At that point

Figure 9.22:
With its air brakes
out XH562 of No. 44
Sqn is here landing
back at Waddington
after an Air Display
on 31 May 1976
(AEO on the aircraft
was Flt Lt
Hathaway). Notice
that the aircraft has
received the Passive
ECM (RWR) on the
tail fin along with
the red/blue national
markings. It no
longer has the black
radome but the
underside of the air-
craft has remained
'white'. Both XM649
and XM602 of No. 9
Sqn can be identified
in the background.
(Lincolnshire Echo)

XL389 of the Waddington Wing had yet to be attached to an individual squadron. It is possible that this aircraft could have been utilized by No. 44 Sqn, but only until June when it was allocated to No. 9 Sqn. A further aircraft, XL445 of No. 35 Sqn, was then attached to the Waddington Wing for four months from 16 June to 1 October 1977. On 6 July 1977, XH562 was initially flown to St Athan for a major service before being issued to No. 230 OCU at Scampton on 27 September 1977. Three days later the OCU transferred XL386 to Waddington (30 September) were it was destined to join No. 44 Sqn. Earlier in the September XL388 had returned to the squadron increasing its total to eight aircraft (XL386, XL388, XM573, XM594, XM598, XM607, XM609 and XM652), until 3 December 1977 when XM652 was flown to Bitteswell for modifications, which took nine months to complete.

During the Queen's Silver Jubilee celebrations at RAF Finningley in July 1977 (29th and 30th) four Vulcans were positioned on the operational readiness platforms. On one of the days the line up consisted of XM650, XM607, XL389 and XM648 (Nos 50, 44, 9 and 101 Sqns respectively), whilst on the other day it changed slightly to XM650, XL389, XM648 and XM594 (Nos 50, 9, 101 and 44 Sqns). Most of these Vulcans would have been familiar to the crews of No. 44 Sqn as XM650 and XM648 had both displayed their squadron's insignia earlier in the year.

Early in the new year XM594 began to receive a major service followed by a fresh coat of paint at St Athan. This aircraft had returned to Waddington by April looking 'spic and span' and later appeared on static display at the station's Open Day on 17 June 1978. On the same day XM573 of No. 44 Sqn gave the solo display after taking part in the four-aircraft scramble. Later in the year this aircraft had the distinction of being the five hundredth Vulcan to receive a major service at St Athan,

Figure 9.23:
XM607 positioned on the ORP at RAF Finningley, representing No. 44 Sqn during the Queen's Silver Jubilee celebrations on 29–30 July 1977.
(*John Huggon*)

Figure 9.24:
On static display at
the aircraft's home
base, Waddington,
on 17 June 1978 is
XM594 of No. 44
Sqn.
(Author's collection)

Figure 9.24:
On static display at
the aircraft's home
base, Waddington,
on 17 June 1978 is
XM594 of No. 44
Sqn.
(Author's collection)

before returning to No. 44 Sqn on 18 December 1978.

XM652 returned to the squadron on 5 September 1978 but three months later on 6 December it departed again to receive further manufacturer's modifications (completed on 28 February 1979). During 1978 the squadron's allocation consisted of six aircraft but two further Vulcans from No. 35 Sqn at Scampton were attached to the Waddington Wing for a period (XL446, 24 May–31 October 1978 and XH538, 16 August 1978–23 November 1979). By the end of 1978 the squadron's allocation consisted of XL386, XL388, XM573, XM594, XM607 and XM609 (XM657 of No. 101 Sqn was at Nellis AFB during December taking part in Red Flag, indicated as displaying No. 44 Sqn's insignia on its tail).

Over the course of the summer of 1979 there were further comings and goings in the squadron. In May XM607 transferred to No. 9 Sqn and by June XJ784 of that Unit was displaying No. 44 Sqn's insignia. Two Vulcans of No. 50 Sqn were transferred to No. 44 Sqn, beginning with XM599 in June and followed by XM575 during August. During July XL389

Figure 9.25:
XL386 of No. 44 Sqn
on detachment to
Luqa, Malta during
1978. This is the only
'XL' serial aircraft
fitted with the single-
emitter head version
of the 'X band jam-
mer' (about early-to-
mid-1970s). This air-
craft can also be
identified as being
the only one with
two ECM plates
whilst fitted with the
device.
(Richard Triner)

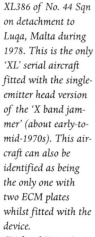

of No. 9 Sqn was transferred to No. 44 Sqn, which allowed XM609 to be sent to Bitteswell on 30 July 1979. At that point XM652 was at St Athan having a major service and was repainted in the new wrap-round camouflage. This aircraft became the first Vulcan to receive the new colour scheme. After serving with No. 44 Sqn for just a month, XJ784 left Waddington for Bitteswell to receive its manufacturer's modifications (9 July 1979–14 May 1980). Although the exact date of transfer is unknown, XM573 had joined No. 230 OCU by 14 August 1979. In September XM652 returned from St Athan and the squadron took charge of XM647 from No. 9 Sqn. The following month XJ824 of No. 230 OCU transferred to Waddington and joined No. 44 Sqn. By the end of October the squadron's allocation consisted of XJ824, XL386, XL388, XL389, XM575 XM594, XM599, XM647 and XM652 (latter aircraft participated in 'Red Flag' at Nellis AFB during December 1979). This allocation reduced when XM599 took its turn at Bitteswell (5 November 1979–15 August 1980).

The youngest Vulcan B.Mk2 XM657, which was now painted in the wrap-round camouflage, had joined No. 44 Sqn by April 1980 and was soon displaying the Unit's insignia on its tail. On 14 May 1980 XJ784 returned from the manufacturers to rejoin the squadron, but by June this aircraft along with XL389 had joined No. 101 Sqn. XM652 was also noted with No. 101 Sqn's insignia for a short period, beginning in June 1980. Over the next two months two more of the squadron's aircraft returned from Bitteswell (XM609, 4 July and XM599, 15 August), then in September it was the turn of XJ824 to go to Bitteswell (19 September 1980–8 June 1981). By the end of 1980 No. 44 Sqn was operating XL386, XL388, XM575, XM594, XM599, XM609, XM647, XM652 and XM657 and the line up remained unchanged for the next six months.

The year 1981 heralded the beginning of the end of the Vulcan Force, with some of the aircraft being stood down even before the individual squadrons disbanded. No. 44 Sqn began the year with the previously mentioned nine aircraft, until 12 March when XM609 was flown to St Athan and declared CAT 5C after flying 5,594.20 hrs. During May XL386 transferred to No. 101 Sqn and XM599 followed XM609 by going to St Athan and also being declared CAT 5C. In June 1981 XJ824 returned from Bitteswell (last Vulcan to do so) and rejoined No. 44 Sqn but by July it had transferred to No. 101 Sqn. No. 44 Sqn had now lost four of its aircraft but it received four others from No. 101 Sqn during July (XM603, XM607, XM612 and XM655). The squadron would therefore have had a total of ten aircraft by August 1981: XL388, XM575, XM594, XM603, XM607, XM612, XM647, XM652, XM655 and XM657.

In September 1981, XM647 transferred to No. 50 Sqn and on

Figure 9.26: *XM575 during its landing run at Waddington on 30 May 1981. Having jettisoned the brake chute, the Land Rover waits close by to collect it from the runway. Notice the tail brake chute door in the open position at the rear of the aircraft. XL361 of No. 9 Sqn is in the background, although it has yet to receive its insignia (displaying No. 35 Sqn's insignia).* **(CBV)**

Figure 9.27: *No. 44 Sqn displaying a number of trophies won in a recent bombing and navigation competition, with XM657 positioned as the backdrop (1981). Notice the rectangular patch around the squadron's insignia on the tail fin indicating the location of the temporary No. 101 Sqn insignia, which it displayed during the Vulcans twenty-fifth anniversary celebrations at Scampton on 25 July 1981.* **(CBV via John Hathaway)**

18 November XL445 of No. 35 Sqn moved to Waddington to join No. 44 Sqn, becoming the fourth Vulcan on the squadron at that point with the wrap-round camouflage scheme (XL445, XM575, XM652 and XM657). The squadron therefore entered into the new year (1982) with nine of the previously mentioned aircraft (August 1981) plus XL445. During the early part of January 1982 XM652 was once again participating in 'Red Flag' (Nellis AFB).

On 12 January 1982 the youngest Vulcan in the RAF departed Waddington on a one-way flight to RAF Manston in Kent. With only 5,100.50 hrs flying time on the clock, XM657's seventeen years service appears somewhat different in comparison with that of XH559's 7,313.15 hrs over twenty-and-a-half years. XM657 arrived at Manston to be placed onto the station's dump for crash rescue training having been allocated this task on the 5th.

After the disbandment of No. 35 Sqn at the end of February 1982, XL319 of that Unit transferred to Waddington to become part of No. 44 Sqn (1 March 1982). The next move occurred on 12 March when XM603 ended its eighteen years of service, when it returned to Woodford to be preserved by some of the very same people that built her. Although the exact date of transfer is unknown, by March 1982 XL388 had moved to No. 50 Sqn after serving with No. 44 Sqn for about seven years.

By the end of March 1982 No. 27 Sqn had disbanded, but two of its B.Mk2 MRRs, with the ability to carry the air-sampling pods, joined No. 44 Sqn. Both XH558 and XH560 were to continue to serve in the MRR role over the following months … 'well, that's what was thought would happen'.

Early in the morning of 2 April 1982, XL388 of No. 50 Sqn made its

Figure 9.28:
After being stationed at RAF Scampton for over twenty years, XL319 was transferred to Waddington at the beginning of March 1982, at which point it was allocated to No. 44 Sqn. The aircraft is being moved from No. 44 Sqn's dispersals, in the background, to the squadron's hangar (1982). During April 1982 ten Vulcans had their flight-refuelling probes reactivated for possible call out to the Falklands, whilst the remainder had them removed in order to equip the C130s and Nimrods. XL319 was possibly one of the ten aircraft originally selected as it still had the probe fitted in June 1982.
(CBV via Craig Jackson)

final flight to RAF Honnington to be placed on the station's dump. Later that afternoon as the members of the crew of XL388 (including the author) returned to Waddington in an RAF Sherpa van, they were welcomed to the sight and sound of XM647 practising for a forthcoming air display. No one at the station on that particular day could have envisaged that the Argentine forces were in the process of capturing the British Colonies of South Georgia and the Falkland Islands in the South Atlantic.

Within days the British Government sprung into action on the political front by attempting to negotiate with Argentina. In the meantime, as if someone had flicked a switch in the RAF, it instantly burst into life planning for the possible call up to mount operations in the South Atlantic. Orders were given several days later indicating that the Vulcans were to play a part in the bombing raids on Port Stanley, the Falkland Islands' main airport. Owing to the volume of Victor tankers that were to be utilized in the South Atlantic, it was also deemed necessary to convert six of the Olympus 201 series Vulcans into single-point tankers as a stopgap for the Northern sector of the UK. Three of the aircraft selected for conversion to K.Mk2 standard were currently operating with No. 44 Sqn (XH558, XH560 and XL445). The squadron was also operating two of the Vulcans that had been selected for the bombing raids (XM607 and XM612). The details of the role and involvement of the Vulcans during the Falkland's Campaign have been covered in great detail in many other publications and therefore I do not feel it is necessary to cover the same ground. By the end of April XM607 and XM612, along with two other Black Buck aircraft, XM597 and XM598, were engaged in the Campaign. This left No. 44 Sqn at Waddington operating XH558, XH560, XL319, XL445, XM575, XM594, XM652 and XM655.

On 25 May XL445 departed Waddington for Woodford to begin the conversion to K.Mk2 standard, followed by XH560 on 15 June and XH558 on the 30th. The squadron by then had been allocated XL427 (early June, ex-No. 50 Sqn) followed, after the Argentine surrender on 14 June, by XM598 (Black Buck Vulcan ex-No. 50 Sqn). By July the remaining two Black Buck aircraft XL391 and XM597 (both No. 101 Sqn) had transferred to No. 44 Sqn to share the Unit's dispersals with XL319, XL427, XM575, XM594, XM598, XM607, XM612, XM652 and XM655.

Throughout the history of the V-Force, Vulcans were regularly detached to Offutt AFB, Nebraska on what was commonly known as 'ranger' missions. On 9 June 1982 a final farewell fly-over of the base took place consisting of six Vulcans. Included in the formation were XL319 and XM575 of No. 44 Sqn. Four days later on 13 June this long-standing tradition came to an end when XL319 became the final Vulcan to depart,

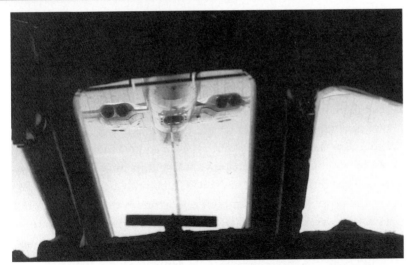

Figure 9.29:
Before being deployed to Ascension to take part in the Black Buck raids on the Falklands, the selected crews had to learn the skills required to take on fuel from the Victor tankers. Notice that the view is limited and the flight-refuelling probe cannot be seen (then imagine this manoeuvre at night!). **(CBV via John Hathaway)**

Figure 9.30:
A rather interesting photograph showing Sqn Ldr Montgomery and his crew (reserve crew for a number of the Black Buck raids) after returning XM607 to Waddington on 20 May 1982. The aircraft is seen after completing two of the bombing raids on Port Stanley Airport, indicated by the two mission symbols on the aircraft's nose (Black Buck 1 and 2). After receiving additional equipment XM607 returned to Ascension to carry out a third bombing raid (Black Buck 7). **(via John Hathaway)**

Figure 9.31:
Black Buck 5 and 6 were carried out to destroy Argentine radar installations on the Falklands. XM597, seen here carrying two Shrike anti-radar missiles, was used on both raids. This is indicated by the two mission symbols on the nose together with a Brazilian flag, which gives reference to its unscheduled landing in Brazil after damaging the flight-refuelling probe. (Capt Sqn Ldr Neil McDougall). **(Crown Copyright/MOD)**

lifting off Offutt's runway and marking the end of an era.

On 13 August XL427 was flown to Mackrihanish in Scotland to be placed on the station's fire dump and XM655 was transferred to No. 50 Sqn. In exchange for XM655, No. 50 Sqn handed over XM569 to No. 44 Sqn during the same month. Also joining the squadron during August was XL360 that came from the recently disbanded No. 101 Sqn.

No. 44 Sqn operated the previously mentioned eleven aircraft until disbanding on 21 December 1982, with the exception of XM652 that transferred to No. 50 Sqn in October.

On 17 December 1982 No. 44 Sqn carried out its last operation launching seven Vulcans in quick succession. Four scrambled from the station's operational readiness platforms followed by the remaining three from the adjacent taxiway. The formation consisted of XM607, XM594, XL360, XL319 (ORP), XM597, XM612 and XL391. The four Black Buck aircraft that participated (XL391, XM597, XM607 and XM612) went on to fly in formation around the ex-Vulcan bases of Coningsby, Cottesmore, Finningley and Scampton before returning to Waddington. Nineteen days later XM607 was flown for the last time (5 January 1983) and in due course it was prepared for static display as the station's gate guard, having completed 5,514.40 hrs. All of the squadron's remaining aircraft were also destined for preservation and were prepared for their final flights over the coming months, with the exception of XM597 that was transferred to No. 50 Sqn on 24 December 1982.

XM598 became the next aircraft to leave the squadron when it was delivered to Cosford on 20 January 1983. The following day XL319 and XM569 were taken on final flights to their new owners. The North East Aircraft Museum in Sunderland received XL319 (6,644.10 hrs) and the Wales Aircraft Museum at Cardiff Airport received XM569 (5,599.40 hrs). One week later on 28 January XM575 joined the Leicestershire Air Museum at East Midland Airport (5,389.30 hrs). The Norwich Aviation Museum received XM612 on 30 January 1983 (5,800.10 hrs) and on 4 February XL360 was delivered to Coventry Airport for the Midland Air Museum (6.467.10 hrs). On a typical wintry day (7 February 1983) XM594 landed at Winthorpe for the Newark Air Museum (5,316.30 hrs). The final aircraft, XL391, arrived at Blackpool for the Manchester Vulcan Bomber Society on 16 February 1983, with only 4,612.35 hrs flown since its first flight in May 1963.

No. 44 Sqn had been the first bomber squadron to convert completely to the Lancaster Bomber in December 1941 and it became the last Vulcan Bomber squadron forty-one years later in December 1982.

Now that all of the Vulcan Bomber squadrons had disbanded it was left to No. 50 Sqn to go it alone as the sole surviving Unit operating the Vulcan, although in a somewhat different role to that of the past (air–air refuelling). No. 50 Sqn continued in this role for a further fifteen months until 31 March 1984.

Figure 9.32:
'ALL DINGOES RUM 50 SQUADRON R.A.F 1918.' This plaque was on display in the squadron's crew room at Waddington in 1982. (CBV)

During the First World War No. 50 Sqn was equipped with Sopwith Camels and used the call sign 'DINGO'. The Dingo, which is a wild, small Australian dog, was painted on the squadron's biplanes and became part of the Unit's insignia in later years. With the reintroduction of Unit markings in 1975, No. 50 Sqn applied two leaping 'Greyhounds', although general opinion appears to be that these were the previously mentioned dingoes. Evidence of this misconception was noted by the author in 1982 on a wall in the squadron's crew room where, among other memorabilia, hung a large oval plaque which consisted of a dark wooden base with three raised brass/copper figurines and a small rectangular etched plate. The three figurines depicted a 'dingo' being chased by two leaping 'greyhounds'. The squadron appears to have dropped the single dingo in favour of the two leaping greyhounds.

Some of the earlier Vulcan B.Mk2s to have this insignia applied during 1975 were XM608 (April), XL387, XM603, XM657 (by the August) and XM654 (by the September). During 1975 XM654 had participated in the Giant Voice Bombing and Navigation Competition against B52s of the USAF whilst displaying the Union Jack on its tail fin along with the two greyhounds. XM654 also retained its black radome and red/white/blue national markings.

By February 1976 XM599 was

Figure 9.33:
No. 50 Sqn's insignia together with the Lincoln coat of arms displayed on XM655 (August 1982–present).
(Author's collection)

now displaying No. 50 Sqn's insignia and the black panther's head of No. 1 Group on the forward fuselage, indicating its previous participation in the Giant Voice Bombing Competition. The Lincoln coat of arms on this aircraft had been applied over the top of a painted rectangular panel that was the previous location of the Union Jack. XM599 had lost its black radome along with the white bib by February 1976.

On 21 April 1976 XM657 was flown to Bitteswell to receive manufacturer's modifications, and in its place received XM597 from No. 44 Sqn. The following month XM651 complimented the strength of No. 50 Sqn when it returned from Bitteswell on 21 May 1976. Helping to increase the numbers still further was XM571 that joined the squadron for five months before returning to No. 35 Sqn (15 June–15 November 1976). By October 1976 No. 50 Sqn was operating XL387, XM571, XM597, XM599, XM603, XM608, XM651 and XM654. On 4 October XM654 made an emergency landing at St Athan after the loss of attitude instruments along with heavy smoke being detected in the cabin soon after take-off. The aircraft then had a multiple birdstrike on landing and the Captain, Flt Lt Lindsay, was awarded a 'Green Endorsement' for the emergency (the aircraft was intended to be flown to Waddington after a major service). Throughout 1976 until March 1977, XM599 is believed to have been with No. 101 Sqn, although the aircraft is understood to have displayed No. 50 Sqn's insignia throughout that period.

In January 1977 XM650 transferred from No. 44 Sqn to join No. 50 Sqn, whilst XM657 returned from Bitteswell before joining No. 101 Sqn two months later (March 1977). By the spring of 1977 No. 50 Sqn was then operating the following eight Olympus 301 series Vulcans: XL387, XM597, XM599, XM603, XM608, XM650, XM651 and XM654. This allocation remained unaltered until 26 January 1978 when XL387 headed to Bitteswell for manufacturer's modifications, which took until 3 November 1978 to complete. The next aircraft of No. 50 Sqn to return to the manufacturers for modification was XM597 (8 April 1978–6 March 1979). During the absence of XM597, the squadron received XM598 from No. 44 Sqn for the same eleven months (April 1978–March 1979). Shortly after XM597 returned to the squadron, XM598 left to receive its own manufacturer's modifications (27 March–24 July 1979). Transferring from No. 101 Sqn in June 1978 was XM575, which remained with it for fourteen months before moving to No. 44 Sqn in August 1979. As previously mentioned, during November/December 1978, XM612 of No. 101 Sqn displayed No. 50 Sqn's insignia whilst at Nellis AFB (Red Flag). At that point in time there were eight other Vulcans already attached to No. 50 Sqn: XL387, XM575, XM599, XM603, XM608, XM650, XM651 and XM654

Figure 9.34:
*XM654 of No. 50
Sqn seen with its
undercarriage
retracting shortly
after take-off at
Waddington on
17 June 1978.*
(John Huggon)

(XM598, major service at St Athan 23 November 1978–26 February 1979).

On 5 February 1979 work began at Bitteswell on XM654 and after the modifications were completed it was returned to No. 50 Sqn (9 November 1979). During May 1979 XM597 moved across to No. 9 Sqn, and No. 50 Sqn received XM605 of No. 101 Sqn in its place. By the end of the next month No. 50 Sqn had been allocated XM569 from No. 9 Sqn, whilst No. 44 Sqn became the recipients of XM599. It was also during June that XM602 (ex-No. 9 Sqn) was noted displaying No. 50 Sqn's insignia (date of transfer unknown). There were further changes before the end of the year when XM575 transferred to No. 44 Sqn in August, followed by XM651 and XM598 that both joined No. 9 Sqn in September/October respectively. Finally in November, XM654 returned from Bitteswell whilst XM603 made the reverse journey to receive manufacturer's modifications (21 December 1979–18 September 1980). On 17 August 1980 XM605 gave a flying display at Kirkbride in its new wrap-round camouflage scheme. By the end of 1979 the squadron was operating the following seven aircraft: XL387, XM569, XM602, XM605, XM608, XM650 and XM654. The squadron's allocation decreased slightly with the transfer of XM602 to No. 101 Sqn in May 1980. After the completion of its manufacturer's modifications on 18 September 1980, XM603 followed in the footsteps of XM602 by joining No. 101 Sqn.

Throughout the next two years the squadron's allocation increased from six aircraft to an eventual total of ten by August 1982. As the Units

Figure 9.35:
Seen during a display at Greenham Common on 23/24 June 1979 is XM605 of No. 50 Sqn. Notice the complete Skybolt attachment points (blisters/fairings) under the wing, along with the four blisters inboard of the large main undercarriage doors indicating the location of the anti-icing unit of the 301 series engines. (QAPI)

of the Scampton Wing disbanded during 1981 and early 1982, more 201 series aircraft were to find their way to No. 50 Sqn.

The squadron's first increase occurred in March 1981 when XH557 transferred from No. 9 Sqn. The following month No. 50 squadron received XL427 (wrap-round camouflage), which also came from No. 9 Sqn. After receiving the previous two aircraft, XM608 made its final flight on 6 April 1981 to St Athan where it was declared CAT 5C and later scrapped. During the final days of service of XM608, it had joined five other Vulcans on a detachment to Bodo (Norwegian AFB), inside the Arctic Circle, for exercise 'Teamwork'. The No. 50 Sqn detachment consisted of XL427, XM608, XM650 and XM654, together with XJ784 of No. 101 Sqn and XM606 of No. 9 Sqn. At the annual Waddington Open Day in May 1981, all seven of the squadron's Vulcans were present and displayed the appropriate insignia: XH557, XL387, XL427, XM569, XM605, XM650 and XM654. Further exchanges took place during September 1981, when XM605 made its last flight to Castle AFB in California for preservation at the Castle Air Museum (5,392.35 hrs). Adding to the squadron's strength in September were XM647 (ex-No. 44 Sqn) and XH561 (ex-No. 35 Sqn, wrap-round camouflage) thereby returning the squadron's allocation to eight. During October XL427 exchanged places with XM598 which returned from its two-year service with No. 9 Sqn (October 1979–October 1981) to serve with No. 50 Sqn once again.

With the disbandment of No. 617 Sqn at the end of 1981, XL426 was allocated to No. 50 Sqn on 5 January 1982 having been flown from Scampton to Waddington the previous day. No. 50 Sqn received a further Vulcan from Scampton on 21 January 1982 in the form of XL321 (ex-No. 35 Sqn). These two aircraft were to take over from XL387 and XM650, which were both declared CAT 5C after being flown to St Athan on 28 January. As previously mentioned the exact date of transfer is unknown, but by March 1982 XL388 (ex-No. 44 Sqn) was operating with No. 50 Sqn. This would have brought the squadron's allocation up to nine aircraft: XH557, XH561, XL321, XL388, XL426, XM569, XM598, XM647 and XM654.

By 25 March 1982 No. 50 Sqn was operating XH557 — 'the oldest Vulcan in service'. The squadron continued to operate XH557 until 10 September 1982 when it was withdrawn from service, but by then it was operating XH558 and therefore retained this title. Before No. 50 Sqn, the previous Unit operating the oldest Vulcan in service was No. 27 Sqn with XH534 (14 August 1974–7 April 1981), followed by XH537 until 24 March 1982.

At the beginning of March, XJ823 was flown to Waddington where its No. 35 Sqn insignia was replaced by an orange 'C' (significance unknown). The following month XL388 made its final flight to Honnington where it was intended to serve on the station's fire dump after flying 5,597.20 hrs (2 April 1982). However, when No. 9 Sqn

Figure 9.36:
The author and four other crew members pose for a photograph at RAF Waddington on the morning of 2 April 1982, before delivering XL388 to RAF Honington on its final flight. The three aircraft in the background are, from left to right: XM647 No. 44 Sqn, XH561 No. 50 Sqn and XM573 No. 9 Sqn.
(Author's collection)

Figure 9.37:
A Tornado GR.Mk1 of the Tactical Weapons Unit at RAF Honington, with Vulcan B.Mk2 XL388 in the background having been temporarily rescued from the dump. Notice the large yellow circle containing a green bat (No. 9 Sqn insignia) painted on the tail fin of the Vulcan.
(Eric Graham via Steven Connor)

reformed as the first Tornado squadron at Honnington in June 1982, the pendulum swung the other way and XL388 was rescued. This aircraft had originally served with No. 9 Sqn during 1962/63 and as a result the squadron's insignia was repainted on the tail fin. At a later date the squadron moved to RAF Bruggen in Germany and as a consequence XL388 was scrapped (the nose section is currently with the Blyth Valley Aviation Collection, Walpole, Halesworth). In the meantime XJ823 had been taken into one of Waddington's hangars on 1 April 1982 and when it re-emerged several days later it displayed No. 50 Sqn's insignia, along with the Lincoln coat of arms.

During April, when the Falkland's Campaign began, the squadron was operating XM598, which was equipped with the original Skybolt attachment points. As a result the aircraft was selected to take part in the forthcoming Black Buck raids on Stanley Airport. The squadron was also operating XH561, which had been selected to become the first conversion to K.Mk2 standard (single-point tanker). XH561 arrived at Woodford on 4 May and made its first flight as a K.Mk2 on 18 June. After the CA clearance had been obtained on 23 June 1982, XH561 was delivered back to No. 50 Sqn on that very same day. Over the next four weeks two further Vulcan K.Mk2s joined the squadron (XJ825 ex-No. 101 Sqn on 1 July and XL445 ex-No. 44 Sqn on 22 July 1982). At the end of the Falkland's Campaign, XM598 was officially allocated to No. 44 Sqn (June 1982). By the end of July, No. 50 Sqn was operating seven B.Mk2s (XH557, XJ823, XL321, XL426, XM569, XM647, XM654) and three K.Mk2s (XH561, XJ825, XL445).

Throughout August No. 50 Sqn received three further aircraft and

Figure 9.38:
Vulcan K.Mk2 XH560 on static display at RAF Mildenhall on 28 May 1983. Notice the Localizer pod mounted next to the main undercarriage door and the two (rectangular) shackles/attachments under both wings hanging from the additional attachment points, outboard and to the rear of the twin Skybolt blisters. Although the air-sampling pods have been removed, the additional blisters (fairings) have not yet been put in place.
(Author's collection)

discarded two of its own. The squadron received from No. 44 Sqn XM655 (in exchange for XM569) followed by the allocation of two K.Mk2 tankers (XH560 23 August and XM571 25 August, ex-No. 44 and 101 Sqn respectively). On 19 August 1982, the service lift of XL321 came to an end when it was flown to RAF Catterick to be placed on the fire dump (6,952.35 hrs). In September two further B.Mk2s were withdrawn from service namely XH557 on the 10th (declared CAT 5C at Waddington), followed by XM647 which was flown (17 September) to RAF Laarbruch in Germany for ground instruction. Both aircraft were eventually scrapped. On 12 October 1982 the sixth and final K.Mk2, XH558, joined No. 50 Sqn. A further B.Mk2, XM654 was withdrawn from service and declared CAT

5C at Waddington on 29 October. By this point XM652 had already transferred from No. 44 Sqn (October 1982). The squadron's total increased to eleven on 24 December 1982 when XM597 joined it following the disbandment of No. 44 Sqn (XH558, XH560, XH561, XJ823, XJ825, XL426, XL445, XM571, XM597, XM652 and XM655). One month later on 24 January 1983, XJ823 made its final flight to Carlisle Airport for preservation by the Solway Aviation Society. This aircraft had been in service with the RAF for nearly twenty-two-and-a-half years and had

Figure 9.39:
Notice the faded squadron insignias of Nos 50, 35 and 27 Sqns on the tail fin of XJ823 at Carlisle Airport (Solway Aviation Society) before the aircraft was repainted.
(Author's collection)

Figure 9.40:
XM597 photographed during an air display at Leuchars on 17 September 1983.
(John Huggon)

clocked up 5,953.30 hrs whilst serving at all six of the Vulcan bases (Akrotiri, Conningsby, Cottesmore, Finningley, Scampton and Waddington). Between 4 and 24 January 1983, XJ823 was under the care of the Holding Flight at Waddington.

No. 50 Sqn continued to operate its remaining ten Vulcans throughout 1983 and early 1984 until being earmarked to disband at the end of March. The complement of ten aircraft consisted of six K.Mk2s (all fitted with 201 series engines) and four B.Mk2s (three fitted with 301 series: XM597, XM652, XM655). They continued to supplement the Victor K.Mk2s in the air–air refuelling role until being superseded by ex-commercial VC10s converted into tankers (*c.*1984). The Vulcan tankers themselves could

Figure 9.41:
XM652 'bows out' after nineteen-and-a-half years of service.
(via John Hemingbrough)

Figure 9.42:
Preserved nose section of XL445 at the Blyth Valley Aviation Collection, Walpole (the nose section of XL388 is in the background).
(Author's collection)

have continued in service beyond 1984 but their Mk17 hose drum units, which were no longer in production, had to be removed and used in the forthcoming VC10 tanker conversions.

Before No. 50 Sqn conducting its final air–air refuelling sortie on 26 March 1984, two of its B.Mk2s were stood down. XM655 made its last flight on 11 February 1984 when it was flown to Wellesbourne Mountford (close to Stratford upon Avon in Warwickshire) for preservation. After some time sitting dormant, XM655 was eventually restored to taxiing condition by a group of volunteers, whose selfless work helped keep memories of the Vulcan Bomber alive. During February XM652 was sold and a month later dismantled, with the intention of being moved by road to a preservation site in Sheffield. After being dismantled the project was cancelled and only the nose section survived, with the remainder of the airframe being scrapped. On 26 March, No. 50 Sqn conducted its final air–air refuelling sortie with XH560 refuelling a number of Tornado and Jaguar aircraft over the North Sea.

On 22 March, four days before this final sortie, XJ825 was allocated for battle damage repair training at Waddington. This aircraft was struck off charge on 5 April and survived on the airfield until being scrapped in January 1992. At the same time as XJ825 was SOC, XL445 made its last flight to RAF Lyneham to serve for a few more years on the station's fire dump for crash rescue training. XL445 survived for a further three years before being scrapped in 1987. Fortunately the aircraft's nose section was recovered and preserved at Walpole, alongside that of XL388 (Blyth Valley Aviation Collection).

On 12 April 1984, the Black Buck Vulcan XM597, which carried out two missions against Argentine radars on the Falkland Islands, made its

Figure 9.43:
Members of the Air
Training Corps pho-
tographed alongside
Vulcan K.Mk2 XM571
under the Rock of
Gibraltar (1984 Gib
Camp, 15–22 August).
Notice the small
'coolant' blister under
the wing. The author,
who is the senior cadet
on the camp (Cadet
Warrant Officer), is
sitting at the end of the
second row, to the left).
(CBV)

final flight to the Royal Scottish Museum of Flight at East Fortune. After being assigned to Waddington's Station Flight in April, XM571 was flown to Gibraltar for preservation on 9 May 1984 but was scrapped in September 1990. The three remaining tankers (XH558, XH560 and XH561) were all initially assigned to the station flight until their demise. The first of these to go was XH561, which joined XH562 and XL321 on RAF Catterick's fire dump on 14 June 1984 to become the fourth Vulcan to end its days there (XH554 ex-No. 230 OCU having already expired by this time). On 17 September 1984

Figure 9.44:
Vulcan K.Mk2 XH561 showing the brake chute door in the open position after the aircraft had just landed at RAF Catterick on 14 June 1984. Notice the hose drum unit, the previous No. 35 Sqn insignia and, in the background, the Hastings on the fire dump.
(Author's collection)

XH558 was taken to RAF Marham's dump, whilst XH560 was retained at Waddington as the reserve airworthy Vulcan Display Team's aircraft. After discovering that XH558 actually had more flying hours available on its airframe than that of XH560, the two aircraft were swapped around. XH558 was allocated to the VDT on 14 November 1984 and XH560 arrived at Marham on 29 November 1984. The latter aircraft survived

Figure 9.45:
A dramatic photograph of XH558 taking off from RAF Leeming on 15 July 1992.
(John Huggon)

Figure 9.46: *A small number of people have played an important role in the preservation of these magnificent aircraft. Lending a hand on the Vulcan Restoration Trust's trade stand are Anne Gardiner, Sarah Gardiner, Linda Penn and Richard Clarkson.* **(VRT collection via Geoff Penn)**

Figure 9.47: *Among the dedicated enthusiasts helping with the preservation of XM655 at Wellesbourne Mountford are Nick Waters, Mark Alcock, Stuart McKechnie, Steve Gleeson, Fred Barter, Derek Hammond and Andrea Mitchell.* **(655 MaPS via Derek Hammond)**

Figure 9.48: *Derek Hammond, right, shaking hands with Sqn Ldr Dave Thomas (Capt), who together with Sqn Ldr Barry Masefield (AEO), standing in the centre, and Wg Cdr Mike Pollit (Co-Pilot), to his right, took XM655 for a fast taxi run down Wellesbourne's runway. On the left is Brian Waters, Managing Director of LSUK, whose company logo appears on the nose wheel door. The firm, like many others, offers valuable assistance in areas such as business, engineering and technical support for the dedicated volunteers/enthusiasts.* **(655 MaPS via Derek Hammond)**

Craig Bulman

until October 1990 at which point it was reduced to scrap, although the nose section survived and is currently preserved. XL426, in the meantime, had been selected as the primary aircraft of the Vulcan Display Team under the command of Sqn Ldr Bill Burnett. The aircraft continued to thrill crowds at air shows around the country from 1984 until 14 June 1986 when it gave its last display at RAF Coningsby, before being replaced by XH558. XL426 made its final journey on 19 December 1986 (6,236 hrs) when it was flown to Southend Airport to be preserved and kept alive by a team of dedicated volunteers. Let us all keep our fingers crossed that one day these people will be rewarded by the sight and sound of this

Figure 9.49:
Andrew Ward like so many other dedicated volunteers is always willing to lend a hand and share his experience with other enthusiasts. He is seen in front of XM655 whilst members of the public take a close look at the aircraft.
(Author's collection)

noble aircraft taking to the skies once again.

XH558 remained with the then Vulcan Display Flight until 23 March 1992 at which point the world's only airworthy Vulcan made its final landing at Bruntingthorpe, Leicestershire, to be maintained in the hope of gracing the skies and enthralling us all in the not too distant future.

After being taken out of service in the early 1980s a number of Vulcans were selected for preservation at various locations in Canada, USA and the UK. Grateful thanks must be expressed to the thousands of dedicated volunteers and supporters from around the world who have given their time, effort and funding in order to preserve these aircraft to this day.

Figure 9.50:
The efforts of all the volunteers are rewarded with the sight of XM655 being put through its paces by Sqn Ldr Dave Thomas (Capt), Co-Pilot Mike Pollit and AEO Barry Masefield. Hopefully one day the ambition of thousands of people may come true with the sight and sound of a Vulcan Bomber taking to the skies once again.
(Author's collection)

Craig Bulman

10

Identification Guide

DESIGNED TO DELIVER BRITAIN'S NUCLEAR WEAPONS to the heart of the Soviet Union, the basic clean, original design of the Vulcan Bomber was modified and adapted in order to take on increasing threats from the perceived enemy. This eventually led to the introduction into service of the Vulcan B.Mk2.

During the production, development and service life of the B.Mk2 numerous features were incorporated, or added at a later date, to the individual aircraft. The fact that no single aircraft received all of the modifications, only a percentage of them, meant that over time numerous permutations developed, making each individual Vulcan or production batch identifiable.

Figure 10.1: A Vulcan being prepared for a night-time sortie at RAF Waddington. Although the aircraft initially appears to be unidentifiable and could be any one of over seventy still in service at that time, by referring to the information given here it is possible to create a short list of just a few. By referring to the chapter that describes this particular era, it then becomes possible to identify the exact Vulcan along with an approximate date that the photograph was taken. (CBV)

This Chapter sets out to identify the individual features along with the modifications and list all the aircraft that received each particular item. Some features were incorporated to all of the surviving aircraft at a particular time and in those circumstances the approximate date that the modification began to appear has been quoted.

ONE OF THE MAJOR ADVANCEMENTS OF THE B.Mk2 over the earlier versions was the increase in power offered by the Bristol Siddeley Olympus 200 series engines. The first of these engines, the Olympus 200, produced 16,000 lb of thrust but with further development and modification the engine produced 17,000 lb of thrust and was known as the Olympus 201. The Olympus 201 series engine initially became the standard fit for the aircraft on the production line, but in order to get the first B.Mk2, XH533, into the air as quickly as possible it was fitted with 200 series engines.

Even before the 201 series had entered service, Bristol Siddeley Engines at Patchway had already began to develop a further Olympus engine that could produce 20,000 lb of thrust. Increased engine power was just what Avro and the RAF were looking for, as increased power would provide an increase in altitude. This new engine would be known as the Olympus 301 series. One problem of this series engine was its overall size, being slightly larger than the 201 series. The Vulcan's engine bays required extensive structural alterations to accommodate the 301 series. This would have been far too costly to retrofit all of the 201 series aircraft. In retrospect this was a wise decision, as eventually the attack profile of the Vulcan changed to low level and the increase in altitude would no longer be a major requirement.

Although the Vulcan's engines are out of sight, it is possible to identify the engine series by the shape of the jet pipe nozzles (exhaust pipes). The 201 series exhaust pipes are longer than those of the 301s, and become narrower as they extend from the trailing edge of the wing. The 301 series on the other hand remains more or less the same width along its length. When the 201 series was first introduced the outer surface of the exhaust pipe was smooth, but in c.1964 several raised square blisters began to be placed around the base of the exhaust pipe. These were required to house the thermo-couplings that no longer fitted into the gap between the exhaust pipe and the new larger diameter jet pipe.

By identifying which of the Olympus series engines are fitted to a particular aircraft (without knowing the serial number) it is possible instantly to reduce the probability of eighty-eight Vulcan Mk2s by about 50%.

If the exhaust pipes are not visible, there is another way to determine the engine series. As mentioned previously the 301 series offered an increase in altitude but at altitude the air temperature is extremely cold.

Figure 10.2:
Although this photo shows the 301 series exhaust pipe, it also shows the location of the thermo-couplings and how they protrude into the jet pipe. **(Author's collection)**

Figure 10.3:
Notice the longer 201 series exhaust pipes on XL392 compared with the shorter 301 series of XM574 (RAF Leeming 16 October 1979). **(Author's collection)**

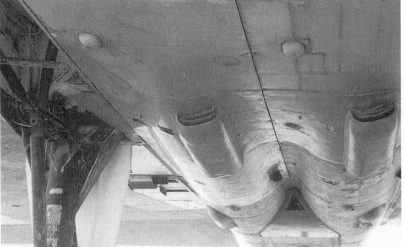

Figure 10.4
(top and middle):
Notice the two blisters/fairings ahead of the engine nestles indicating the location of the exhaust outlet of the anti-icing unit of the 301 series engines.
(Author's collection)

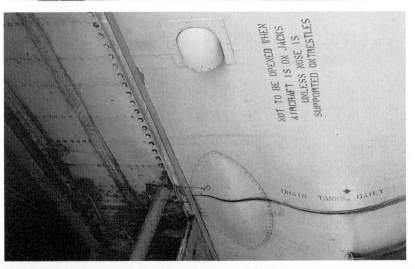

NOT TO BE OPENED WHEN
AIRCRAFT IS ON JACKS
UNLESS NOSE IS
SUPPORTED ON TRESTLES

DRAIN TANKS DAILY

Figure 10.5:
Close-up of the anti-icing unit exhaust blister of the outer engine on the starboard side (looking to the rear). Be careful not to mistake this one with the oval-shaped bulge, which is present on both series of engines (seen directly behind on this photo). The latter is actually the location of the constant drive speed unit.
(Author's collection)

One of the features of the 301 series was an anti-icing unit placed ahead of the engine that prevented ice from forming on the guide vanes, thereby allowing the aircraft to cope with the lower air temperatures at altitude. The external evidence of this is four small dome-shaped blisters with an exhaust outlet to the rear. These can be found ahead of the engine nestles on the flat under surface of the wing, inboard and half way down the length of the main undercarriage bays. If the under surface of the wing remains flat at that point then it is a 201 series aircraft. If the dome-shaped blisters (exhaust) are evident then you have identified a 301 series aircraft.

The following list of aircraft all initially left the Woodford production line fitted with the **Olympus 201 series** engines. For identification purposes the earlier Vulcans fitted with the 200 series engines are incorporated into the following list:

XH533	XH561	XL320	XL426
XH534	XH562	XL321	XL427
XH535	XH563	XL359	XL443
XH536	XJ780	XL360	XL444
XH537	XJ781	XL361	XL445
XH538	XJ782	XL384	XL446
XH539	XJ783	XL385	XM569
XH554	XJ784	XL386	XM570
XH555	XJ823	XL387	XM571
XH556	XJ824	XL388	XM572
XH557	XJ825	XL389	XM573
XH558	XL317	XL390	
XH559	XL318	XL392	
XH560	XL319	XL425	

(total of 53)

Out of this allocation of 53 aircraft, nine in due course were to be retrofitted with the Olympus 301 series engine. The first of these to be selected was XH557, which became the test bed and trials aircraft for the 301 series engine. Initially this aircraft flew with only one of these engines fitted (19 May 1961) whilst retaining three of its original 201s. It later received a second (both port engines) before finally receiving all four. The second Vulcan B.Mk2 to be selected by Avro to have its engine bays modified to accept the Olympus 301s and assist with their development was XJ784 (April 1962). The remaining seven aircraft all came from the same serial batch and were retrofitted with the 301 engines when they were returned to Woodford, after each serving with the RAF for about eighteen months (1962–64). The retrofits and return to service dates of these aircraft (XL384, XL385, XL386, XL387, XL388, XL389 and XL390) are all quoted in Chapter II.

Prior to the Olympus 301 series engine becoming fully established on the Woodford production line a single aircraft, XL391, had them incorporated into its engine bays. It also received the complete Skybolt attachment points and was delayed on the production line for about ten months whilst this additional work was carried out. It was then delivered to the Ministry of Aviation, 22 May 1963 to participate in trials of the 301 series engine and the Skybolt missile. There have been numerous reference sources describing aircraft fitted with 301 series engines as having the designation of B.Mk2A. The reference B.Mk2A is a myth; regardless of the engine series these aircraft have the designation B.Mk2.

Taking the previously mentioned ten aircraft into account, the following list consists of all the Vulcan B.Mk2s fitted with the **Olympus 301 series** engines:

XH557	XM575	XM604	XM647
XJ784	XM576	XM605	XM648
XL384	XM594	XM606	XM649
XL385	XM595	XM607	XM650
XL386	XM597	XM608	XM651
XL387	XM598	XM609	XM652
XL388	XM599	XM610	XM653
XL389	XM600	XM611	XM654
XL390	XM601	XM612	XM655
XL391	XM602	XM645	XM656
XM574	XM603	XM646	XM657
			(total of 44, i.e. 50%)

Figure 10.6:
*An aircraft fitted
with 'one' ECM plate
(XL443 of No. 27
Sqn seen during a
display at Plymouth
in 1971).*
(Colin. J. Dodds)

ONE OF THE STANDARD FEATURES of the Vulcan B.Mk2, also adopted by the B.Mk1s when converted to B.Mk1A standard, was the flat plate aerial fitted between the two starboard jet pipes. This flat plate was used to mount additional ECM aerials such as the Red Shrimp jammers (two or three small dome-shaped aerials) and/or the 'L' band aerial (large rectangular blade aerial).

Although this single flat ECM plate was the 'standard' fit for B.Mk2s coming off the Woodford production line, some of the aircraft that were selected to carry the Blue Steel missile received a second ECM plate between the two port jet pipes. This second plate appears to have been fitted after they had entered service, although a small number may have had them fitted from the start. Some Blue Steel Vulcans fitted with the two ECM plates occasionally had two additional aerials mounted on the port ECM plate. These two aerials were larger than the Red Shrimp jammers positioned on the starboard plate and they appear as two small wedge-shaped blisters on the port side only, e.g. XL388, XL444, XL446, XM571, XM572, XM594 and XM595. All of these ECM devices mounted onto either of the flat plates were interchangeable, the two wedge-shaped blisters on the port side appear to have been removed from all of the aircraft once they reverted to conventional bombing.

Of the aircraft that received the second ECM plate, some were fitted with Olympus 201 series and some with 301 series engines. The combination of engine series and the number of flat ECM plates creates further permutations, e.g. 201-one, 201-two, 301-one and 301-two.

Figure 10.7: *Seen at Finningley whilst operating with No. 230 OCU during 1966 is XL444 (Trouble Four). Notice the two additional wedge-shaped blisters positioned on the port ECM plate (above the stepladders at the rear of the aircraft).* **(APN)**

Figure 10.8: *Starboard ECM flat plate aerial used to mount additional devices such as Red Shrimp (dome-shaped) and the 'L' band aerial.* **(Author's collection)**

The following list consists of all the Vulcan B.Mk2s fitted with **two ECM plates (1962–64)**. The last aircraft fitted with the two plates was XL390 whilst receiving a retrofit during 1964/65 (re-entered service in May 1965):

XL318	XL385	XL444*	XM572*
XL319	XL386	XL445*	XM573*
XL320	XL387	XL446*	XM575*
XL321	XL388	XM569*	XM576*
XL359	XL389	XM570*	XM594*
XL384	XL390	XM571*	XM595*

(total of 24).

Note: the aircraft in the first two columns originally had only one ECM plate. Until further evidence becomes available it remains unknown if the aircraft in the remaining columns initially entered service with one or two plates fitted (*all known to be fitted with two by 1964).

The following list consists of all the Vulcan B.Mk2s equipped with only **one ECM plate** during their **'complete service life'**:

XH533	XH563	XL427	XM610
XH534	XJ780	XL443	XM611
XH535	XJ781	XM574	XM612
XH536	XJ782	XM597	XM645
XH537	XJ783	XM598	XM646
XH538	XJ784	XM599	XM647
XH539	XJ823	XM600	XM648
XH554	XJ824	XM601	XM649
XH555	XJ825	XM602	XM650
XH556	XL317	XM603	XM651
XH557	XL360	XM604	XM652
XH558	XL361	XM605	XM653
XH559	XL391	XM606	XM654
XH560	XL392	XM607	XM655
XH561	XL425	XM608	XM656
XH562	XL426	XM609	XM657

(total of 64)

ORIGINALLY BLUE STEEL was intended to be a preliminary weapon pending the introduction into service of the Skybolt nuclear missile. When the latter missile was cancelled, the RAF had to continue with Blue Steel for longer than expected. After equipping three squadrons with twenty-six Blue Steel aircraft (eight each and two spare), a further seven aircraft were converted increasing the overall total of Blue Steel-equipped Vulcans operated by the Scampton Wing to thirty-three. Chapter II describes the reason why these additional seven aircraft were required. There have been numerous reference sources describing aircraft equipped with Blue Steel as having the designation B.Mk2A. The reference B.Mk2A is a myth; aircraft equipped with Blue Steel still retained the designation B.Mk2.

The following list consists of all of the Vulcan B.Mk2s **modified to carry Blue Steel**:

XH539	XL384	XL426	XM572
XL317	XL385	XL427	XM575
XL318	XL386	XL443	XM574
XL319	XL387	XL444	XM575
XL320	XL388	XL445	XM576
XL321	XL389	XL446	XM594
XL359	XL390	XM569	XM595
XL360	XL392	XM570	
XL361	XL425	XM571	

(total of 34).

Figure 10.9:
XL443 equipped with a Blue Steel missile whilst giving a display at Biggin Hill (possibly 1969/70).
(Colin. J. Dodds)

Note: XH539 never entered squadron service (trials aircraft only).

Craig Bulman

Figure 10.10: *On the leading edge of both wings are two very small rectangular patches. It is in the area directly behind these that the combination of blisters/fairings would exist. Notice on this early production Vulcan B.Mk2 (possibly Biggin Hill c.1961) the smooth underside of the aircraft's wing (no blisters).* **(Colin. J. Dodds)**

THE NEXT AREA TO OBSERVE in order to assist identification is on the underside of the wing, outboard of the main undercarriage doors. It is in this location that several different combinations of blisters appear, or in a number of cases the lack of them. The blisters indicate the location of the wing hard points on which it was intended to mount pylons to carry external stores such as Skybolt missiles.

As previously mentioned Skybolt was intended to be the main weapon carried by the Vulcan B.Mk2, but the first priority was to establish the B.Mk2 into squadron service as quickly as possible. The second priority then became to introduce Blue Steel (intended preliminary weapon only) and achieve an operational status with at least one Squadron. The third task would then have been to supersede Blue Steel with Vulcans powered by Olympus 301 engines (increased altitude) equipped to carry Skybolt.

As the first two priorities did not require the wing hard points, due to the fact that Blue Steel would be mounted semi-recessed in a new bomb bay fairing, the first batches of Vulcan B.Mk2s all emerged from Woodford with the under surface of the wing remaining smooth (no blisters).

The following list consists of all the Vulcan B.Mk2s that came off the production line with **no blisters on the underside of the wing**, outboard of the main undercarriage doors:

XH533	XH560	XL318	XL390
XH534	XH561	XL319	XL392
XH535	XH562	XL320	XL425
XH536	XH563	XL321	XL426
XH537	XJ780	XL359	XL427
XH538	XJ781	XL360	XL443
XH539	XJ782	XL361	XL444
XH554	XJ783	XL384	XL445
XH555	XJ784	XL385	XL446
XH556	XJ823	XL386	XM569
XH557	XJ824	XL387	
XH558	XJ825	XL388	
XH559	XL317	XL389	

(total of 49).

Note: in due course all of the above-mentioned XH and XJ serial aircraft were retrofitted with the twin (Skybolt) blisters in *c.*1964/65, with the exception of four of the earlier trials aircraft (XH533, XH535, XH539 and possibly XH536).

Two blisters under the forward wing, outboard of the main undercarriage doors, indicate the forward attachment point of the Skybolt missile pylon. The rear attachment point is indicated by a single dome-shaped blister situated in alignment with the forward two blisters, at approximately the centre of the aircraft's wing. A smaller dome-shaped blister appears immediately in front of the forward attachment point (twin blisters). This smaller blister is believed to be the refrigeration ducting required to provide the missile with coolant. During the Falkland's War this blister appears to have been used for the electrical cable required

Figure 10.11 (left and opposite page): *Three views showing the necessary combination of blisters/fairings required for mounting and operating the Skybolt missile. Notice in the top photo the two black patches on the leading edge of the wing and the 'coolant' blister ahead of the forward attachment points (twin blisters). The dome-shaped blister indicates the rear attachment point, which can be seen more clearly in the second photo (looking forward). The third photo taken from the side shows the forward attachment points and the coolant blister.* **(Author's collection)**

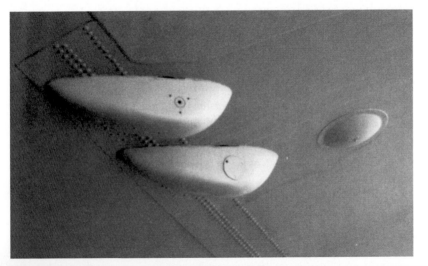

for the Shrike missiles and additional ECM pods.

Pending the introduction into service of the Skybolt missile Avro allocated XH537 and XH538 to the Ministry of Aviation in order to conduct trails in connection with the missile. XH537 first flew with two dummy missiles in an attempt to discover the aerodynamics and handling of the missiles in November 1961. We understand that XH538 conducted powered launches of the missile, as opposed to the drops made from XH537. The latter aircraft appears to have been used to assess the aerodynamics of the missile, which may account for the lack of the additional small (coolant) blister ahead of its twin attachment points. In January 1961 a further Vulcan B.Mk2, XH563 of No. 83 Sqn, flew to the Douglas plant at Santa Monica, California to conduct electrical compatibility tests (Douglas being the producer of the Skybolt missile).

The following list consists of all the Vulcan B.Mk2s fitted with the **'complete' Skybolt attachment points**:

XH538	XM600	XM605	XM610
XL391	XM601	XM606	XM611
XM597	XM602	XM607	XM612
XM598	XM603	XM608	
XM599	XM604	XM609	

(total of 18)

Figure 10.12:
XM594 is one of only nine aircraft to have been fitted with the small 'coolant' blister only. Notice the saddle-shaped fuel tank on the floor beneath the bomb bay.
(Author's collection)

Before the first batch of Vulcans came off the production line with the 'complete Skybolt attachment points' a number of aircraft appeared with only the small (coolant) blister under their wings.

The following list consists of all the Vulcan B.Mk2s fitted with the **small (coolant) blister only**:

XM570	XM573	XM576
XM571	XM574	XM594
XM572	XM575	XM595

(total of 9)

The following list consists of all the Vulcan B.Mk2s fitted with the **Skybolt attachment points, but lacked the small (Coolant) blister**:

XH537

By the time the Skybolt missile project was cancelled in November 1962, work on fitting the hard points to the Vulcan B.Mk2s on the production line had already commenced. Owing to the cancellation of the missile, the remaining Vulcans on the order book were completed with only the front attachment points, as indicated by the twin blisters. As mentioned previously the earlier XH and XJ serial Vulcans currently in service were to be retrofitted with the same twin (Skybolt) blisters (*c*.1964/65).

What seems unusual is that if the missile was **cancelled in November**

Figure 10.13:
Notice on XH537
(Finningley
17 September 1966)
the twin Skybolt blisters and the single dome-shaped blister, indicating the front and rear attachment points for the Skybolt missile pylon (aircraft lacks the coolant blister).
(John Hemingbrough)

Figure 10.14:
Close-up of the twin Skybolt blisters showing their location in relation to the two black patches on the leading edge of the wing.
(Author's collection)

1962 and the complete attachment points were no longer fitted, why were the earlier XH and XJ serial aircraft retrofitted with the twin blisters two-to-three years later (1964/65)? Possibly they were intended for something other than Skybolt that we have yet to be told about! Even so, these blisters are normally referred to as the '**twin Skybolt blisters**'.

The following list consists of all the Vulcan B.Mk2s fitted with the twin Skybolt blisters:

XH534	XH561	XJ823	XM650
XH554	XH562	XJ824	XM651
XH555	XH563	XJ825	XM652

XH556	XJ780	XM645	XM653
XH557	XJ781	XM646	XM654
XH558	XJ782	XM647	XM655
XH559	XJ783	XM648	XM656
XH560	XJ784	XM649	XM657
			(total of 32)

WHEN NO. 27 SQN REFORMED in November 1973 to perform a new role of Maritime Radar Reconnaissance, it began to receive a modified version of the B.Mk2 known as the B.Mk2 MRR (sometimes incorrectly referred to as SR.Mk2, an easy mistake to make as these aircraft replaced the Victor SR.Mk2s of No. 543 Sqn). Delivery of these modified Vulcans took place over the next four-and-a-half years.

The following list consists of all of the Vulcan B.Mk2s converted to perform the role of MRR and received the designation of **B.Mk2 MRR**:

XH534	XH560	XJ782
XH537	XH563	XJ823
XH558	XJ780	XJ825

(total of 9)

Some of these aircraft were equipped with **additional hard points** during conversion in order to carry air-sampling pods as well as a smaller 'localizer' pod. The air-sampling pods were mounted slightly outboard and slightly to the rear of the twin (Skybolt) blisters, whilst the localizer pod was positioned under the port wing outboard of the main undercarriage door. When the pylons/pods were removed they were replaced by a number of small blisters. Those that covered the air-sampling pod attachment points consisted of two small blisters at the front and a smaller single blister to the rear. When the 'localizer' pod was removed a single small blister replaced it.

Figure 10.15:
The underside of the port wing of XH558 showing the additional blisters that indicate the location for mounting the localizer and air-sampling pod. Notice that a large number of access panels have been removed.
(Andrew Edmondson)

The following list consists of all the Vulcan B.Mk2 MRRs equipped to carry the air-sampling pods and have the appropriate combination of **'additional blisters'**:

XH534
XH537
XH558
XH560
XH563

(total of 5).

Note: notice how they are all 'XH' serial B.Mk2 MRRs.

An additional feature of the B.Mk2 MRRs was two small white-blade aerials positioned on top of the aircraft's nose. These appear to have been added *c.*1975/76. Some of the aircraft equipped with these two blade aerials were selected during 1982 to be converted into K.Mk2 tankers. During their conversion at Woodford the two aerials were removed.

The following list consists of all the Vulcan B.Mk2 MRRs and B.Mk2s fitted with the **two white-blade aerials** on top of the nose:

XH534	XH560	XJ782	XL361
XH537	XH563	XJ823	
XH558	XJ780	XJ825	

(total of 10)

Figure 10.16:
The two white-blade aerials fitted to the aircraft adapted to perform the role of maritime radar reconnaissance (XJ823).
(Author's collection)

Figure 10.17:
When the Terrain-Following Radar was removed from the aircraft it was replaced by a circular fairing/cap. The Vulcan depicted is XJ782, B.Mk2 MRR. Notice that the refuelling probe has also been removed (Finningley 1983).
(Craig Jackson)

Figure 10.18:
Having delivered XL388 to RAF Honington on 2 April 1982, two crew members are seen walking away from the aircraft for the final time. Notice the black fairing/cap placed on the tip of the aircraft's nose.
(Author's collection)

Figure 10.19:
XH554 was one of the Vulcans that never received the Terrain-Following Radar, notice that the tip of the nose remains smooth and the camouflage extends around the nose, in comparison with the two previous photographs (RAF Catterick 1983).
(Author's collection)

A FURTHER RECOGNIZABLE FEATURE of the B.Mk2 MRR was the absence of the Terrain-Following Radar from the tip of the aircraft's nose. The radar began to appear in 1966 and was fitted to most of the surviving aircraft over the following two years. This item of equipment was detachable and when removed a circular 'cap' replaced it. Some of the Vulcans, however, were never equipped with the radar and on these aircraft the tip of the nose remains smooth, with the upper and lower camouflage extending around the nose.

The following list consists of all the Vulcan B.Mk2s and B.Mk2 MRRs **never equipped with Terrain-Following Radar**:

XH533	XH537	XH556	XM576
XH534	XH539	XH559	XM601
XH535	XH554	XH563	
XH536	XH555	XL385	

(total of 14).

Note: it is unknown whether XM604 received the radar before it crashed in January 1968.

DURING 1965 A VULCAN B.MKIA, XA907, of the Bomber Command Development Unit began trials with a device known as the 'X band jammer'. The device was fitted to the underside of the aircraft's tail, positioned on the forward ECM bay inspection door and was recognizable by a single-emitter head facing rearwards. Assisting in the trials of the X band jammer was Vulcan B.Mk2 XH538 (1965–67). XH538 retained this single aft-facing emitter head throughout its service life until being stood down in 1981. This device helped to complement the Vulcan's existing ECM fit in an attempt to jam further Soviet threats such as airborne radars and therefore prevent detection. The X band jammer began to appear on some of the Cottesmore Wing aircraft (Olympus 301 series only) during 1967. The remainder of the Wing's aircraft received it after being transferred to the Waddington Wing the following year. In c.1972 each of the B.Mk2s had the single-emitter head unit replaced by an improved version with two emitter heads. The new unit now had two

Figure 10.20: XH538 became the first B.Mk2 to receive the single-emitter head version of the 'X band jammer' (aft-facing) fitted below the tail section. The aircraft is seen landing at RAF Lakenheath in June 1970. **(APN)**

Figure 10.21: Beneath the Vulcan's bulged ECM tail section there are three inspection doors, notice how the 'X band jammer' is mounted on the forward door. This photograph shows XM655 fitted with the newer version consisting of two emitter heads. **(Author's collection)**

Figure 10.22:
All of the 301 series aircraft (XM597–657) fitted with the 'X band jammer' had an additional dome-shaped fairing (significance unknown) placed on the under-side of the fuselage, ahead of the bulged ECM tail section shown here on XM655.
(Author's collection)

aerials, one facing forwards and the other facing rearwards. Two further Vulcan B.Mk2s received the single-emitter version of the X band jammer during the 1970s and coincidentally both of them (XH559 and XL386) were operating, or had been operating, with No. 230 OCU.

The following list consists of all of the Vulcan B.Mk2s fitted with the **X band jammer (single-emitter head only):**

XH538	XM602	XM610	XM652
XH559	XM603	XM611	XM653
XL386	XM605	XM612	XM654
XM597	XM606	XM648	XM655
XM598	XM607	XM649	XM656
XM599	XM608	XM650	XM657
XM600	XM609	XM651	

(total of 27).

Note: it is unknown whether XM604 received this unit before it crashed in January 1968.

An important fact to note about the above list is that the first three aircraft of the final serial batch (XM645, XM646 and XM647) did not have this item fitted. For possible reasons for the absence of this unit on these three aircraft, see Chapters I, V and IX.

During the winter months of 1984/85 XH558 was being converted back to a B.Mk2 at RAF Waddington, after serving with No. 50 Sqn as a K.Mk2 tanker from 1982 to 1984, in preparation to take over from XL426 of the Vulcan display team. Part of the work involved the removal of the hose drum unit from the aircraft's tail and replacing it with the three ECM bay inspection doors. These doors obviously came from another aircraft that had previously been part of the Waddington Wing as the forward door still had the 'X band jammer' housing attached.

The following list consists of all the Vulcan B.Mk2s fitted with the **X band jammer that had two emitter heads** facing forward as well as rearward (1972 onwards):

XM597	XM605	XM612	XM653
XM598	XM606	XM648	XM654
XM599	XM607	XM649	XM655
XM600	XM608	XM650	XM656
XM602	XM609	XM651	XM657
XM603	XM611	XM652	XH558*

(total of 23).

*Total increases to twenty-four if you choose to add XH558 to the count. Note: XH558 only had this unit attached whilst it was a display aircraft (1986–present). Whilst at the Norwich Aviation Museum, due to damage, the forward ECM bay inspection door was replaced on XM612 (no longer has the X band jammer unit fitted).

(See colour Plate 10) DURING THE MID-1970s the Vulcans began to take on a new look with the addition of passive ECM (Radar Warning Receiver) mounted on top of the tail fin. This unit had originally been tested on XM597 of the Waddington Wing between November 1971 and February 1973. All of the surviving Vulcans in service from 1975 received this new look (universal by the end of 1977).

The following list consists of all the Vulcan B.Mk2s and B.Mk2 MRRs fitted with the rectangular look, **passive ECM tail fin**:

XH534	XL318	XL445	XM608
XH537	XL319	XL446	XM609
XH538	XL320	XM569	XM611
XH554	XL321	XM570	XM612
XH557	XL359	XM571	XM645
XH558	XL360	XM572	XM646
XH559	XL361	XM573	XM647
XH560	XL386	XM574	XM648
XH561	XL387	XM575	XM649
XH562	XL388	XM594	XM650
XH563	XL389	XM595	XM651
XJ780	XL390	XM597	XM652
XJ782	XL391	XM598	XM653
XJ783	XL392	XM599	XM654
XJ784	XL425	XM602	XM655
XJ823	XL426	XM603	XM656
XJ824	XL427	XM605	XM657
XJ825	XL443	XM606	
XL317	XL444	XM607	

(total of 74).

Note: it remains unknown whether XM600 received this device before crashing on 17 January 1977.

BEGINNING SEPTEMBER 1979 a number of Vulcan B.Mk2s were repainted with the new wrap-round camouflage after receiving a major service at St Athan. The pattern of camouflage on the aircraft's upper surface was repeated on the underside, with dark sea grey replacing the original medium sea grey. This change came about through experience gained during the participation of the USAF's realistic warfare exercise 'Red Flag' during 1977 and 1978.

The following list consists of all the Vulcan B.Mk2s that received the **wrap-round camouflage**:

XH558	XL389	XL444	XM648
XH561	XL425	XL445	XM652
XL318	XL426	XM575	XM657
XL359	XL427	XM605	

(total of 15).

Note: XH558 received this colour scheme with an additional 'glossy' finish during September–November 1985 at RAF Kinloss, before becoming the display aircraft for the Vulcan Display Team in May 1986.

Figure 10.23: Beginning in September 1979 all Vulcans sent to St Athan for a major service were painted in the wrap-round camouflage scheme. XL427 is seen at the end of its flying career at RAF Macrihanish in 1982 before being placed onto the fire dump. (CBV)

Figure 10.24:
*Vulcan K.Mk2 XJ825
of No. 50 Sqn refu-
elling a Tornado
GR.Mk1 of No. 9
Sqn.* **(CBV)**

DURING 1982 A NUMBER OF VULCANS powered by Olympus 201 series engines were selected for conversion into single-point tankers. These aircraft were to supplement the Victor K.Mk2s in the air–air refuelling role until the introduction into squadron service of the VC10 tankers. There was a short-fall of tankers in the UK as most of the Victors were at Ascension engaged in operations in connection with the Falkland's Campaign.

The following list consists of all of the Vulcan B.Mk2s and B.Mk2 MRRs converted into **K.Mk2 single-point tankers**:

XH558	XJ825
XH560	XL445
XH561	XM571

(total of 6)

IN ADDITION TO ALL OF THE PREVIOUS FITTINGS and modifications that help identify an individual aircraft or production batch, there are other features that can provide information to ascertain an approximate date. A number of these features/modifications were fitted or applied as standard and appeared on all of the aircraft within one or two years, but some of the other modifications took longer to appear. By identifying an appropriate era and with reference to the previous Chapters, it is possible to ascertain which aircraft were allocated to a particular Unit or Wing during that time.

Figure 10.25:
At first glimpse this aircraft, XJ823, appears to have been photographed at any time during the 1960s or early 1970s (centralized servicing era). By looking at a number of features around the airframe and then finding the appropriate references within this Chapter, it is possible to determine the approximate year. A reference to this aircraft, identifying the date and location, appears in Chapter 1. (APN)

Craig Bulman

Figure 10.26:
*Notice how the air-
craft's serial number
is repeated on the
exhaust covers
(XL443 Finningley,
17 September 1966).
(John
Hemingbrough)*

FIRST, IF THE SERIAL NUMBER on the aircraft's tail fin is not visible, it may still be possible to identify the individual Vulcan by looking at other parts of the airframe where the same serial number occasionally appears. These areas include the inside of the main undercarriage doors, the outside surface of the nose wheel doors (bottom left/right corners) and the bottom outside edge on the rearward-facing door behind the main undercarriage. The serial number of the aircraft sometimes appears on the air intake covers or on the circular covers placed inside the aircraft's exhaust pipes. With regard to the latter, these covers are usually padded with two cloth handles and were normally painted silver. The detail on each can vary by displaying the squadron number, different individual letters, e.g. G/F/J, or the serial number of the appropriate aircraft. The latter method of identification cannot be taken for granted due to the fact that the covers can be removed and occasionally used by other Vulcans of the same engine series. It has also been noted that a set of covers has the serial numbers of two different aircraft displayed at the same time. An example of this was in the mid-1960s when the set of covers on an aircraft of the Scampton Wing displayed the serial number of XL388, whilst an additional darker patch placed just above showed the serial number of XM574 (both 301 series).

ONE OF THE EARLIEST CHANGES TO OCCUR was the addition of **air–oil separators**, which were placed along the side of the engine nestles. These consisted of a single external pipe on each of the four engines (mounted between each pair of engines), although if ECM plates are fitted these can only be seen from the rear. The air–oil separator pipes appear to have first been introduced during **1962** and appear to have become universal by the **end of 1963**.

Figure 10.27:
Notice the air–oil separator pipes situated between the port engines of XJ823. (Author's collection)

Craig Bulman

Figure 10.28:
*Notice the Loran
antenna (long, thin
aerial) on the port
nose wheel door of
XJ823 No. 50 Sqn.
The aircraft is shown
whilst on static dis-
play at the Teesside
Air Show on
28 August 1982.*
(Author's collection)

ONE OF THE NEXT CHANGES TO OCCUR was in **1964**, when a long, thin aerial was placed on the port nose wheel door. This item is understood to be the **Loran antenna**. Some of the first aircraft to receive this item were still in their white colour scheme at that time. Most, if not all, of the aircraft appear to have been fitted with this aerial by the end of **1965**. During that time some of the aircraft had received their low-level camouflage, but had yet to be fitted with the aerial. It has been noted on at least one occasion that an individual aircraft, having previously been fitted with this aerial, had been identified with the item temporarily removed. Although the telltale oval-shaped patches indicating the two mounting positions showed that the aircraft concerned had already been equipped with the device.

ALSO DURING **1964** THE SMALL PROTRUSION that was situated beneath the aircraft's tail, just in front of the tail lamp (navigation light) was modified. The item in question was the **tail bumper**, which protected the aircraft's tail (to a certain degree) when the nose of the plane was held too high during landing/take-off. The new design, which was slightly larger than its predecessor, incorporated a metal probe extending beneath a metal housing. If the probe made contact with the runway it would give the pilot a warning in the cockpit in order for him to take the appropriate action. The original tail bumper was painted either black or white, however when the new tail bumper was introduced it was always painted the same colour as the aircraft's underside (white during the 1960s). This item appears to have been universal by the end of **1965**.

Figure 10.29:
The modified tail skid/bumper was introduced during 1964. Notice the navigation light to the rear of the tail bumper fairing.
(Author's collection)

Figure 10.30:
The shape and location of the large, red anti-collision light covers can clearly be seen in these two photographs.
(Author's collection)

ONE ITEM THAT CAN EASILY BE TAKEN FOR GRANTED is the red dome-shaped cover placed over the top of the anti-collision lights. Three appear around the aircraft with two positioned under the wing in front of the lower air brakes. The third is positioned on top of the fuselage beside a very small blade aerial situated behind the two larger communication aerials. However, these three large, **red dome-shaped anti-collision light covers** did not appear until *c.*1966 and seemed to be universal by the end of **1968**.

WHEN THE VULCAN B.MKIS WERE CONVERTED to B.Mk1A standard they received two additional aerials. These are understood to be VHF communication aerials, with the first of them positioned on top of the fuselage, midway between the rear of the cockpit canopy and the similar but slightly larger existing communication aerial. The second aerial was mounted under the aircraft's nose on the bomb-aiming blister. These two aerials that both sloped to the rear became a standard fit on the B.Mk2, with the exception of the early production aircraft with the B.Mk1 pointed tail cone and XH534 when it first flew during 1959. These earlier aircraft eventually received the two aerials, together with the larger communication aerial.

During the early 1970s the two small VHF aerials were replaced by a modified version that could be identified by its more uniform shape and colour (vertical/yellow). Initially these aerials all appear to have been painted yellow, but at a later date some of them had a single black line painted across their centre. Although the shape is important the colour is not a good identification feature, as at any given time an individual

Figure 10.31:
XL320 of the Scampton Wing at Kia-Tak, Hong Kong on 17 April 1969. Notice the location, top and bottom, of the two VHF aerials. **(CBV via Rod Powell)**

Craig Bulman

Figure 10.32:
*XL386 of No. 44 Sqn
seen in 1978 at Luqa,
Malta. Notice the
more vertical and
uniform shape of the
modified VHF
aerials.*
(Richard Triner)

aircraft could have any combination of the two styles. The modified yellow VHF aerial began to appear during the second half of **1970**. One of the first aircraft noted with these aerials was XM653 in September 1970. This modification appears to have become universal by the **Autumn of 1975**. One of the last Vulcans to have been noted with the old style aerials was **XL317 in May 1975**.

POSITIONED ON THE PORT SIDE of the aircraft's nose, ahead of the canopy and approximately half way down the fuselage, is the emergency equipment stowage and destruction bay. When the Vulcan B.Mk2 first entered service with its anti-radiation white colour scheme, the symbols displayed on the panel (axe, fire extinguisher and gloves) were painted with a **pale red 'outline'**. On aircraft that were involved in trials and displaying darker national markings, however the symbols in the majority of cases were painted completely **red** not just outlined. One of the exceptions was XH537 displaying dark national markings but pale red outlined symbols (c.1962). In the bottom right-hand corner of this panel there was a solid **red cross** indicating the location of the first-aid kit. Positioned to the right of this panel was a vertical lever that would be pulled in emergency to release the canopy. This emergency release handle, along with all of the appropriate written instructions for both the equipment bay and the release handle, were also painted red/ pale red at that time.

Figure 10.33: *Photographed at RAF Gutersloh, Germany on 26 May 1967 are, from left to right, an unknown German Air Force Officer, Sqn Ldr Pete Odling (Capt), Flt Lt Briggs (Co-Pilot), Flt Lt Dave Flynn (Nav Plotter), Flt Lt Wilks (Nav Radar), Fg Off Ken Drummond (AEO), Ch Tech Austin and Ch Tech Pierce. The members of the crew, all from No. 230 OCU at Finningley, were at this location to participate in a flying display with XH555. Notice the yellow symbols and other stencilling on the emergency equipment bay panel together with the 'white square' background for the first-aid cross. XH555 had recently been returned to the OCU from St Athan, having just been repainted and in doing so became one of the first to display the 'white square' background. (****Crown Copyright****)*

With the introduction of low-level camouflage onto the upper surface of the aircraft during **1964**, the three symbols on the equipment bay were painted **yellow**, although some appear to have been painted with a yellow outline only. Also a large **yellow arrow with a black outline** and the word 'RESCUE' painted in black was placed on the side of the fuselage pointing at the previously mentioned vertical lever (emergency canopy release).

The next alteration to these symbols began to appear on individual aircraft during **1967** when a **'white square'**-shaped background was placed behind the red first-aid cross, in the bottom right-hand corner of the emergency equipment bay. One of the earlier examples of this was XM656 at the approximate time of its transfer from the Cottesmore Wing to the Waddington Wing. The **white square background** was slowly introduced as standard over the following years and appears to have become universal by the end of **1972**. The aircraft appear to have received the 'white square' after having a major service and a complete re-paint, and in the majority of cases a more solid outline was applied to the new camouflage.

IN THE UNFORTUNATE EVENT of a Vulcan coming to rest on its belly, for example if the undercarriage failed to lower, the emergency crews may need to gain access to the fuel or weapons within the bomb bay to make them safe. This was made possible by the fitting of a **bomb bay inspection panel**. The panel was on the upper port surface of the fuselage, about half way along the shallow leading edge of the tail fin. Although the panel had always existed, there was very little external evidence of its location. During the 1960s, a broken line and a written description in the centre, all painted yellow, indicated the panel's location; an example of these markings was displayed on XL360 during 1968 whilst operating in the Blue Steel role. At a later date, a white circle containing the words 'FOAM LANCE' indicated the centre of the panel, together with 'break in here for bomb bay inspection' painted above/below in yellow. This more obvious marking of a white circle first began to appear during **1969**. Some of the first Vulcans displaying this 'white circle' were XM647 of the NEAF in July 1969 and XH563 in September 1969 whilst it was on loan to the Ministry of Technology. This particular marking appears to have been universal by the end of **1971**.

Figure 10.34:
The important point to note here is the 'white circle' painted on the upper fuselage below the shallow part of the tail fin. The white circle indicates the location of the bomb bay inspection panel (XL443, possibly at Biggin Hill, 1969/70).
(Colin. J. Dodds)

Figure 10.35:
*XM595 of No. 617
Sqn giving a display
at Turnhouse on
26 June 1971. Notice
the large black panel
on the port wing,
outboard of the
engine nestles and to
the rear of the under-
carriage doors. This
panel is the location
for the Doppler
radar.*
(John Huggon)

THROUGHOUT THE **1960s and early 1970s** all of the Vulcan B.Mk2s were
noted with a large flat panel (dark in colour) situated directly behind the
port main undercarriage doors. The panel was the location for the
Doppler radar, which *c.1972* began to be modified and appeared as a
raised square unit in the middle of the original panel. The square-shaped
Doppler radar is understood to have become universal by **1974**.

Figure 10.36:
*XM594 of No. 44
Sqn believed to be
giving a display at
Abingdon on
12 September 1981.
Notice that the large
black panel for the
Doppler radar has
been replaced by a
much smaller square-
shaped unit placed in
the centre of the orig-
inal panel. (CBV)*

Figure 10.37:
XL387 and XM612 of the Waddington Wing are poised ready to scramble at Finningley on 8 September 1973. XL387 has the red/blue national markings together with the light grey underside, but has retained the white on the rear of the radome (bib). Only these two Vulcans are understood to have participated in the scramble demonstration on this occasion.
(John Huggon)

DURING **1972** THE PROCESS BEGAN to tone down the red/white/blue national markings by omitting the white. One of the first Vulcans to be seen with the new low-visibility **red and blue roundels** was XL427 of No. 230 OCU. These red and blue roundels appear to have been universal by the end of **1975**. One of the last Vulcans noted with the red/white/blue roundels was XM652 of the Waddington Wing. When the aircraft were repainted with a matt finish and light grey underside, the yellow **symbols on the emergency equipment bay were painted in red**. Before the aircraft were repainted, some Vulcans received the red and blue roundels but retained the yellow symbols and glossy colour scheme (e.g. XM649 in 1974). The red/blue roundels were initially applied to the aircraft's port wing only, but they began to be painted on to the **starboard wing in 1973** (e.g. XL387 and XM646). The **two**, red/blue roundels on the aircraft's wings appear to have become **universal by 1977**. Two examples noted with only one upper wing roundel in August 1976 were XH534 of No. 27 Sqn and XL317 of No. 617 Sqn.

A further change occurred with the Vulcan's colour scheme during **1974** when the camouflage was extended over the black radome. The first Vulcan known to display this new look was XM651 of the Waddington Wing, when it appeared at RAF Finningley for the annual Battle of Britain Day in September of that year. The black radomes seamed to have disappeared by the end of **1976**. Some of the last Vulcans to display their black radomes during 1976 were XJ784, XJ825, XL388 and XM646.

WHEN THE VULCAN B.MKI ENTERED SERVICE it was equipped with a brake parachute, which deployed out of the starboard side of the small pointed tail cone. When the bulged ECM tail of the B.Mk1A was introduced, the brake chute housing was relocated in the top of this new section and can be identified by a predominant blister consisting of a forward fairing and a parachute compartment door. After using the tail brakechute the only means of closing the compartment door was to climb above it and wind it shut with a special tool. The shear awkwardness of this operation combined with the height required to reach the door proved to be dangerous and a number of accidents occurred. At a later date a new and safer method was devised which allowed access to the brake chute door from the underside of the aircraft, via the rear ECM bay inspection door, to winch it shut. To make this operation possible a raised metal winching point was placed on the outside of the parachute compartment door on its rear edge. The raised metal **winching point** first began to appear in **1974**. An early example of this was XH538 of No. 27 Sqn (April 1974).

Figure 10.38:
Notice the raised metal 'winching point' on the rear edge of the parachute compartment door of XL427, at Macrihanish in October 1985. Note the absence of the Red Steer tail radome.
(Author's collection)

DURING THE VULCAN'S CAREER a number of aircraft participated in bombing and navigation competitions against the USAF. These aircraft generally had a Union Jack and/or No. 1 Group's panther's head insignia on the tail fin/fuselage and appeared in numerous permutations. Aircraft noted with the **panther's head on the fuselage only** whilst displaying red/white/blue roundels were XM600, XM607 and XM650 (red/blue roundels, XM599* and XH563*). Those noted with the **Union Jack on the tail fin only** whilst displaying the red/white/blue roundels were XJ781, XL392 and XM654. The only Vulcan noted so far with **both of the markings** whilst retaining the red/white/blue roundels was XM602 (red/blue roundels, XM599, XM606, XM649, XM653 and XM655). In September 1973 XM606 was noted with the Union Jack having a 'white' outline and the Lincoln coat of arms on the tail fin whilst on a visit to Sao Paulo in Brazil (panther's head on fuselage). All of the aircraft mentioned in this paragraph still had a black radome at that point in time, with the exception of XM599* and XH563* (latter aircraft received the panther's head during 1982 whilst preserved at Scampton).

During the late 1970s XH538, XL387, XL388, XL445 and XM571 were all noted with the **panther's head painted beneath the Union Jack on the tail fin**. Similar markings were noted on XM605 with its wrap-round camouflage when it was flown to Castle AFB for preservation in October

Figure 10.39: *Whilst serving with the Vulcan Display Flight, XL426 displays the Union Jack on the tail fin and the panther's head on the fuselage. (Author's collection)*

Figure 10.40:
*Whilst preserved at
Scampton (1982–86),
the panther's head of
No. 1 Group was
applied to Vulcan
B.Mk2 MRR XH563.*
(Terry Quinn)

1981. The two Vulcans used by the VDT/VDF (1984–92), XL426 and XH558 displayed the Union Jack on the tail fin and the panther's head on the fuselage.

OVER THE YEARS VULCANS HAVE BEEN SPOTTED with numerous markings, official and unofficial. One of these, the triangular **'squadron commander's pennant'** used to identify the CO's personal aircraft, was painted in pale blue/red on the **forward fuselage**. This form of identification occurred during the early 1960s whilst the aircraft were still in their white colour scheme. When No. 83 Sqn first operated the B.Mk2 the commanding officer of the squadron, Wg Cdr R. Davenport, selected XJ782 as his personal aircraft. At the end of 1962 when No. 83 Sqn was in the process of being equipped with the Blue Steel missile, the new squadron commander, Wg Cdr J. Slessor, selected XL426 to display the 'pennant'. Ten months after taking command of the squadron, Wg Cdr Slessor achieved an unofficial record of 'four hours five minutes' from Goose Bay in Canada to RAF Scampton whilst flying XL426 (10 September 1963). Four days later the same aircraft was on display to the public when it appeared at the annual Battle of Britain Day at RAF Finningley as part of the scramble demonstration along with three other Vulcans from the same squadron (XL425, XL392 and XL443). The second Unit to be equipped with the B.Mk2 was No. 27 Sqn under the command of Wg Cdr V. Cramer, who selected XJ823 as his personal aircraft. The third Scampton Unit to equip with the B.Mk2 was No. 617 Sqn in September 1961, commanded by Wg Cdr L. G. A. Bastard until superseded by Wg Cdr H. Currell in November 1962. The aircraft on the squadron selected to display the 'pennant' was XL321. At RAF Coningsby during 1963, Wg Cdr P.J. Lagesen, who was No. 12 Sqn's Commanding Officer, is understood to have displayed the pennant on XH560. During the 1970s, the Commander's Pennant appeared on the following two aircraft, XL427 No. 230 OCU, c.1973 and XM612 No. 101 Sqn (late 1970s whilst participating in Red Flag at Nellis AFB).

Figure 10.41: *XJ823, as seen during 1961/62 with No. 27 Sqn's Indian elephant insignia on its tail fin and the commander's pennant on the fuselage, to the right of the roundel here (Waddington September 1961).* *(APN)*

Craig Bulman

ANOTHER FORM OF IDENTIFICATION that appeared on a number of Vulcans was the introduction of several 'stars' painted on the fuselage above the crew entrance door (significance unknown). **During 1962 XL321** of No. 617 Sqn displayed a **single** white star on a pale blue square background. This item was positioned next to the squadron badge on the **forward fuselage**. The same aircraft is understood to have displayed a **single** white star on a blue square background during 1973 whilst operating with No. 230 OCU. At the end of 1963 and during 1964 XJ824 had a pale blue rectangle with **three** white stars painted on the forward fuselage, midway between the side observation window and the crew entrance door (No. 230 OCU Finningley). The same aircraft was noted with **four** blue stars painted immediately above the entrance door at the time it served with No. 44 Sqn during late 1979 and early 1980. During 1982 XJ823 of No. 50 Sqn was also noted with the **four** stars above the entrance door. In the late 1970s whilst operating with the OCU at

Figure 10.42:
Four blue stars (significance unknown) painted above the crew entrance door of XJ823 (1982).
(Author's collection)

Scampton, XH562 displayed **two** of these stars. A second aircraft, XL360, of the same Unit (*c.*1976/77) displayed **two** white stars on a dark rectangular background, positioned 'immediately' below the green camouflage above the crew entrance door. During its final year of service, XL319 of No. 44 Sqn had a **single** star painted above the entrance door and XM605 (wrap-round camouflage) displayed **two** of them on a white rectangular background whilst on display at Castle AFB in 1982.

IN ADDITION TO ALL OF THE PREVIOUS INFORMATION, there is one final point that makes each Vulcan uniquely different and identifiable from any other. From 1964, each aircraft received the **'same pattern'** of green/grey disruptive camouflage onto the upper surface of its wings and fuselage. One of the first B.Mk2s to receive the camouflage was XM645 in March **1964** and one of the last aircraft noted was XL425 in early **1965**. The only exceptions to this were XH533, XH535 and XH539, which remained white throughout their life span. Even though the pattern of the camouflage remains the 'same' on all of the aircraft, the individual curves and widths are **'uniquely different'**. By comparing the individual pattern with other reference sources available, it is possible to determine the identity of the aircraft. The way to look upon it is to think of each aircraft having its own **'fingerprint'**, but it is important to take into account the fact that each Vulcan was **repainted several times** during its time in service. Using this method there are other important points to be aware of. First, after receiving repairs to various parts of the airframe or obtaining a different squadron's insignia for example, the appropriate section would have been repainted, slightly changing the 'fingerprint'. Second, replacement parts such as the aircraft's rudder, ailerons/elevators (elevons), cockpit canopy, tail radome (Red Steer), for example, occasionally came from other aircraft and retained their colour scheme for a while. Finally, because of the curvature of the fuselage and wings, the same section of camouflage can look very different if it is viewed from a different angle.

Figure 10.43:
Why not put your knowledge to the test and try to identify the following Vulcans. *Knowing that the first picture was taken in September 1981, it is possible to identify the individual aircraft serial number.*
(Craig Jackson)

Figure 10.44:
Knowing that this picture was taken in 1979, it is possible to reduce the probability to just two aircraft. With additional reference sources it is possible to identify the individual aircraft by the pattern of camouflage and the position of the squadron insignia.
(Author's collection)

Figure 10.45: *After initially studying the picture it is possible to create a short-list of just four aircraft.* *(Colin J. Dodds)*

Figure 10.46: *Try to identify these two Vulcans at RAF Catterick out of the following four: XH554, XH561, XH562 or XL321?* *(Author's collection)*

Figure 10.47:
*After studying this
photo it is possible to
identify the aircraft
and also determine
the approximate date
(within two months)
when the photo was
taken.*
(Author's collection)

THE DATES QUOTED WITHIN THIS BOOK showing the transfer or allocation
of an aircraft from one Unit to another may differ slightly from the
actual date that the physical movement occurred.

Bibliography

A GREAT DEAL OF RESEARCH and cross-referencing of information had to be carried out to portray as accurately as possible the integration and service history of the individual Vulcan B.Mk2s. Many books and publications have also been read to achieve this:

Alan Baxter, *Olympus — The First Forty Years* (Rolls Royce Heritage Trust, 1990)

Andrew Brookes, *Avro Vulcan* (Ian Allan, 1985)

——, *V Force: The History of Britain's Airborne Deterrent* (Jane's, 1982)

Duncan Cubit and Ken Ellis, *Vulcan: Last of the V-Bombers* (Osprey Aerospace, 1993)

Kev Darling, *Avro Vulcan* (Specialty Press and Wholesalers, 1999)

Bob Downey, *V-Bombers* (Arms and Armour, 1985)

Paul Jackson, *Wings of Fame*, vol. 3 (Aerospace Publ., 1996)

Robert Jackson, *Avro Vulcan* (Patrick Stephens, 1984)

——, *V-Bombers* (Ian Allen, 1981)

Tim Laming, *V-Bombers* (Patrick Stephens, 1997)

——, *The Vulcan Story* (Arms and Armour, 1993)

Philip J. R. Moyes, *Bomber Squadrons of the RAF and Their Aircraft* (Macdonald & Jane's London)

Jim Simpson, *RAF Gate Guards* (Airlife, 1992)

Alan Todd, *Vulcan Photo Album* (Control Column Publ., 1987)

Vulcan, Aeroguide 6 (Linewrights, 1984)

Stewart Wilson, *Vulcan Boeing B47 & B52* (Aerospace Publ., 1997)

Humphrey Wynn, *RAF Nuclear Deterrent Forces* (HMSO, 1997)

655 News

Air-Britain Digest

Air Enthusiast

Air Forces International

Air Pictorial

Aircraft Illustrated

Airshows

FlyPast

Journal of Military Aviation

The Official Journal of the Vulcan 558 Club

RAF News

Roundel

Vulcan News

Warbirds Illustrated

Index